P9-AOV-240

Advent,
Christmas,
and Epiphany

BRIAN WREN

Advent, Christmas, and Epiphany

LITURGIES *and* PRAYERS *for* PUBLIC WORSHIP

Westminster John Knox Press
LOUISVILLE • LONDON

© 2008 Brian Wren

All rights reserved. Except as provided in the "Reproduction Guidelines" on p. ix, no part of this book may be reproduced or transmitted in any form or by any means, electronic or mechanical, including photocopying, recording, or by any information storage or retrieval system, without permission in writing from the publisher. For information, address Westminster John Knox Press, 100 Witherspoon Street, Louisville, Kentucky 40202-1396.

Scripture quotations, unless otherwise indicated, are from the New Revised Standard Version of the Bible, copyright © 1989 by the Division of Christian Education of the National Council of the Churches of Christ in the U.S.A., and used by permission. Some Scripture quotations are modified or simplified. See the introduction, p. xi.

Scripture quotations marked REB are taken from *The Revised English Bible,* copyright © Oxford University Press and Cambridge University Press, 1989. Used by permission.

The publisher is grateful to all who have granted permission to use songs they control. Individual notice of such permission is given below the songs. See p. ix for information about which songs, liturgies, and prayers may be reproduced for use in congregational settings without seeking further permission.

Book design by Drew Stevens
Cover design by Lisa Buckley

First edition
Published by Westminster John Knox Press
Louisville, Kentucky

This book is printed on acid-free paper that meets the American National Standards Institute Z39.48 standard. ∞

PRINTED IN THE UNITED STATES OF AMERICA

09 10 11 12 13 14 15 16 17 — 10 9 8 7 6 5 4 3 2

Library of Congress Cataloging-in-Publication Data

Wren, Brian A.
   Advent, Christmas, and Epiphany : liturgies and prayers for public worship
/ Brian Wren.
— 1st ed.
      p. cm.
   Includes indexes.
   ISBN 978-0-664-23309-9 (alk. Paper)
   1. Advent—Prayers and devotions.   2.   Christmas—Prayers and devo-
tions.   3.   Epiphany—Prayers and devotions   4.   Worship programs
I. Title.
   BV40.W47 2008
   264—dc22

                                                                2008010817

To Hilary and Nicholas Wren,
my daughter and son,
whose faith journeys
nourish and inspire my own

Contents

Items marked Years A, B, or C are for general use but designed also to go with the Revised Common Lectionary (RCL).

Acknowledgments

Many people have helped to make this book possible. Sabbatical leave granted by the Trustees of Columbia Theological Seminary in the autumn of 2004 enabled me to lay the groundwork and compose materials for Advent and Christmas. The love and prayers of the seminary's leadership and faculty colleagues helped make it possible for me to complete the work during the final semester before my retirement. Students in many places helped me develop and sharpen my methods and theology. Friends and colleagues reviewed and used early drafts. I am grateful in particular to Lindsay P. Armstrong (Presbyterian Church, U.S.A.); Dan Damon (United Methodist Church, U.S.A.); Warren McDougal (United Church of Canada); William Middleton (Presbyterian Church in Canada); Martha Moore-Keish (Presbyterian Church, U.S.A.); John Martin (Uniting Church in Australia); Shirley and John Murray (Presbyterian Church, New Zealand); Leigh Olson (United Church of Canada); Donald Rudalevige (United Methodist Church, U.S.A.); Larry E. Schultz (Pullen Memorial Baptist Church, Raleigh, North Carolina); Richard Smith (United Church of Christ, U.S.A.); Carolyn Smyth (United Reformed Church, U.K.); Diana Townsend (United Reformed Church, U.K.); Alida Ward (United Church of Christ, U.S.A.); and Mary Weber Hall (United Methodist Church, U.S.A.).

An author prepares a work, but many hands and minds are needed to improve it and make it ready for publication. I am grateful in particular to Barbara Fehl, who cast her eagle eyes over the manuscript, and to the editorial and production team of Westminster John Knox Press, for their encouragement, skill, and dedication at every stage.

My partner in marriage and ministry, Susan Heafield, is my primary and best critic and has been my indispensable colleague and friend in the preparation of this work.

Reproduction Guidelines

To make this book user-friendly, permission is given to reproduce the prayers and liturgies free of charge in noncommercial congregational worship materials, such as printed or projected orders of worship, subject only to the following conditions:

> *All such items must be reproduced without alteration, omission, or addition* to protect their integrity as published and to prevent alterations from getting into circulation. The following notice must be printed at the end of the printed order of worship that includes such item(s) or be projected on screen beneath the item(s) or in a separate slide : "TITLE(S) OF ITEM(S) is/are from Brian Wren, *Advent, Christmas, and Epiphany: Liturgies and Prayers for Public Worship* (Louisville, KY: Westminster John Knox Press, 2008) and are reproduced by permission. Copyright © 2007 by Brian Wren."

The three worship songs by Susan Heafield and Brian Wren printed in chapter 1 ("Someone Comes," "Great Holy One," and "Rejoice! Give Thanks") may be reproduced in worship free of charge on the same terms and conditions as the prayers and liturgies. Use the copyright notices printed in chapter 1. The songs are from *We Can Be Messengers: Worship Songs—Christmas, Before and After,* by Susan Heafield and Brian Wren (book and CD), available from Hope Publishing Company (U.S.A.) or Stainer & Bell (U.K.). See Web references below.

Permission is needed from the publishers to reproduce hymns owned by Hope Publishing Company and in the U.K. by Stainer & Bell, and their ownership of particular hymns in this volume is clearly noted. For U.S.A., Canadian, Australian, and New Zealand rights, contact Hope at www.hopepublishing.com. For other rights, contact Stainer & Bell at www.stainer.co.uk. For both publishers, permission can also be obtained by using a OneLicense or CCLI license. CCLI and OneLicense cover a wide range of hymns and songs in different musical styles by many music publishers and are recommended for congregations (not choirs) that wish to sing copyrighted hymns and songs. For CCLI, visit www.ccli.com/. For OneLicense, go to www.onelicense.net/.

Introduction

This book is for Christian public worship in any size of group or congregation. It consists of orders of worship (liturgies) and worship elements, including calls to worship, collects, litanies, thanksgivings, confessions of sin, and affirmations of faith for use in worship during the four weeks before Christmas (Advent), Christmas, and after Christmas as far as the first Sunday in the New Year (Epiphany).

The Sundays in Advent together with Christmas Eve, Christmas Day, and New Year's Eve/Day are high points in the Christian calendar, and there is a continuing need for worship resources. This book tries to meet the need with material that is theologically sound, creative, Scripture oriented, and crafted to encourage vigorous and rhythmic public utterance. Each item is original, and almost all are published here for the first time.

Some of the liturgies are for use within a congregation's own order of worship, for example, the Hanging of the Greens and the lighting of Advent candles. At Christmas, three complete Services of Scripture and Song offer fresh alternatives to the King's College Cambridge Service of Lessons and Carols.

The worship elements in this book are suitable for a variety of worship traditions and are intended for use within a congregation's customary order of worship. Some items are best spoken by a worship leader on behalf of the congregation; some can be spoken by a congregation; and others can be spoken responsively by two or more worship leaders or by leader and congregation. Each item is prefaced by a brief explanation of how it can most appropriately be used.

In order to expand the worship repertoire still further, each section of the book includes a selection of my hymn and song lyrics, some of which are not available in hymnals. The music of these hymns can be accessed on the publisher's Web site. To make the material user-friendly, permission is given to reproduce the prayers and liturgies free of charge in noncommercial worship materials, such as printed or projected worship orders. Hymns have different requirements, but permission to reproduce them is inexpensively obtained. (See p. ix.)

Theme Based or Lectionary Based?

Many congregations choose Scripture readings to follow particular Scripture narratives or themes or to hear complete books of the Bible. Many others follow the Revised Common Lectionary (RCL), which provides Scripture readings and a psalm for every Sunday in the Christian Year and covers significant portions of the Bible during its three-year cycle (Years A, B, and C).

Advent, Christmas, and Epiphany is intended for both types of congregation. All the worship materials in this book are compatible with the RCL days and readings listed. RCL users will find prayers and other liturgical elements for every Sunday from Advent to Epiphany in all three lectionary years.

In the Advent to Epiphany season, congregations not committed to the RCL are nonetheless likely to use a number of its Scripture selections, such as the nativity narratives in Matthew and Luke and the "messianic" sections of Isaiah and the Psalms. The Scripture index points the way to materials drawn from such passages, while the topical index lists items usable on other occasions during the year. The book is Scripture based and Scripture oriented: every item is drawn from or prompted by an RCL reading.

Approaching Scripture

Prayers and other worship elements described as from, drawn from, prompted by, echoing, or responding to a Bible passage have varying degrees of relationship to it, including paraphrase, partial quotation, and language intended to honor but not imitate it. I have sometimes given chapter-and-verse, sometimes not.

Readings from the Bible and references to it are mostly from the New Revised Standard Version (NRSV), an ecumenical translation that has been widely adopted and improves greatly on previous revisions of the historic King James (Authorized) Version.

To take one example, the NRSV recognizes that many occurrences of Hebrew and Greek words literally meaning male human beings or male siblings were not addressed to all-male audiences or communities but to audiences or communities of women and men—and sometimes, also, children. When the apostle Paul calls his recipient congregations literally "brothers," he is merely following linguistic convention and clearly intends to include both genders. Thus, where the original has such words, formerly and elsewhere rendered "men" or "brothers," the NRSV makes a more accurate translation by using terms such as "mortals," "human beings," and "brothers and sisters."

I have sometimes amended the NRSV in the interests of liturgical flow—for example by dropping the occasional "and" to improve speech rhythms—and by shortening or taking extracts from some quotations in the Advent Candles liturgies, where the aim is to mark an essential element in the source, not hear its full exposition. I have also simplified or amended the NRSV on occasion and marked the reference with an asterisk (*) to indicate that I have done so or have included my own translation. I have avoided divine pronouns (God as "he," "him," etc.) out of the conviction that English pronouns are more gender laden than their Hebrew and Greek antecedents and that biblical voices know that the Creator of male and female cannot be either.

More noticeably, perhaps, I have used nonmale alternatives to the word "Lord" throughout this book in quotations from the Hebrew Bible (Old Testament). To put the matter briefly, the word "LORD" or "the LORD" is not a *translation* of the Hebrew Name of God but instead translates a word spoken *in place of that divine Name.* In Hebrew the noun in question has the consonants

"YHWH" (perhaps originally pronounced "Yahweh") and seems to be a proper name as distinct from a title such as Shepherd, Rock—or God. By the time of Jesus, the Name "YHWH" had long been avoided in prayer and in readings from Scripture. Other words were substituted for it, such as "Elohim" (God) or most commonly "Adonai" (chieftain, governor), for which the equivalent in the England of King James was the aristocratic male rank and title "Lord." Though nowadays archaic, "Lord" still carries associations of maleness and male dominance absent from the name "YHWH." Though "Adonai" is a common substitution in Jewish worship, few Christian congregations currently use it. I have, therefore, sought other substitutions, such as "Living God" or Holy One." Sometimes I have used another Jewish substitution, "the Name" (Hebrew *Ha-Shem*).[1]

In some scripture quotations, the source is announced in general terms (e.g., "Listen to these words from the Gospel of John" on p. 4, and the chapter-and-verse reference is printed at the end in italics (*John 1:1–5 and 8–12**). A reference like this is best left unspoken, so as not to impede the flow of worship. In this particular case the asterisk indicates that I have modified the NRSV to express a Greek word that means both "understand" and "overcome." Similarly, when two or more Scriptures sources are quoted without interruption (e.g., Isa. 7:14 and Matt. 28:20 on p. 35), the chapter-and-verse references are printed but unspoken. In readings where chapter-and-verse is printed at the beginning, the speaker announces it.

Praying from This Book

The prayers and worship elements in this book will hopefully come alive by being spoken. Because we live in a visual culture, please look for ways of using video and images to give more depth to the words.

Most types of prayer will be familiar or self-explanatory. *Pastoral prayers* typically incorporate *adoration, praise, thanksgiving, confession of sin, petition* (asking God's help), and *intercession* (praying for others)—categories that also occur separately along with other kinds of utterance (e.g., *affirmation of faith, meditative* (*informal*) *prayer, call to prayer, charge,* and *blessing* (*benediction*). A litany is a series of prayers with the same repeated response (see p. xv below). A collect (pronounced "COLL-ect") aims to collect or sum up a congregation's prayers. Collects have the classic Anglican form, as in the following for Epiphany Sunday (see p. 199):

Toddler Christ,	(*Address—who are we speaking to?*)
whose light shines out,	
not from a palace,	
but from a village woman's lap,	(*Ascription—more about "who"*)
shine on us today	(*Petition—one specific request*)

1. A more complete discussion of "LORD" is in my book *Praying Twice: The Music and Words of Congregational Song* (Louisville, KY: Westminster John Knox Press, 2000), 243–52.

through the youngest and the least,
that we may open our treasures   (*Purpose—The hoped-for result*)
and give them precious gifts   (*Close—Ending the prayer*)
in your name. Amen.

Ecstasy and Economy

In many (not all) Pentecostal and Black American traditions, public prayer is ecstatic—an outpouring of praise, petition, lament, and intercession with vocal congregational participation. When congregation and preacher are steeped in the King James (Authorized) Version of the Bible, the preacher can draw on that knowledge so that the prayer becomes an unscripted Scripture-laden utterance.

At the other end of the spectrum, public prayer in Anglican (Episcopal) and Lutheran traditions tends toward economy. It is mostly or often Scripture based; highly scripted; screened prepublication for theology, brevity, clarity, and speech rhythms; and spoken from a printed worship order, prayer book, or other service book. When scripted prayers are internalized, they can sometimes be spoken without thought. Alternatively, their very familiarity can prompt intense awareness.

Scripted, unscripted, economic, ecstatic—the boundaries shift and blur. Psalms 34, 103, and others are scripted but impassioned. Some people steeped in Anglican and Lutheran traditions can utter new unscripted collects, perfectly formed.

Economic and ecstatic prayers have one important thing in common. Like the biblical prayers from which they are ultimately derived, they originate in an intensely oral culture, where prayer was chanted or spoken and in the best sense publicly "performed." Their natural habitat is as speech spoken and heard, not a text read silently on a page or grudgingly grumbled in a classroom.

Obviously, the prayers in this book are scripted. Some tend toward economy. Others, I hope, are touched with the ecstatic. They risk being dead in the water if treated with—dare I say it—Methodist mumble or Presbyterian plod. To bring the prayers to life as committed public speech, try the following teaching moves and action strategies:

1. Periodically remind one another that in our culture, public speaking by a group is an uncommon activity outside church. *To speak together in worship is therefore countercultural.* Not perhaps objectionable, but certainly a little odd. We do it not out of habit but for good reason—because we belong together in Christ and by speaking with conviction together we commit ourselves publicly to Christ and to one another. This being so, it's important to speak out—not to shout, but not to mumble either.
2. When we speak aloud together, we do not speak for ourselves alone. We speak also for those who cannot join in, for whatever reason: literal speechlessness, grief, loss, heartache, disappointment, depression, or hurt. We

voice a faith some long for but do not yet have, a trust that some are as yet unable to share, and a hope that we ourselves perhaps go in and out of, but which belongs to the whole company of Christ's people.

3. Resist market anxiety—the culturally conditioned consumerist impulse to make every prayer, every Sunday, "new" and "different"—even if very rarely "improved!" Worship thrives on familiarity as well as on innovation. So choose a few prayers from this book and repeat them over several weeks until they become familiar. Then, if they can also be used at other times of the year, revisit them periodically.

4. When using a short prayer such as a Collect, sometimes ask the congregation to read it over silently for a few minutes and quietly say it to nonreaders or sight-impaired neighbors—and then to speak it together (not "read it") from the heart.

5. Ask a choir or form a speaking team to lead/perform some of the litanies, such as "By God's Generous Love" (p. 162) or "God Alone, Through Jesus Christ" (p. 171), to demonstrate how they sound as committed public utterance. Optionally have the congregation sing or say the response.

Format and Typeface

The worship elements and liturgies in this book are formatted in short lines rather than spread out in prose paragraphs across the page. This format is intentional and important. Whether spoken by one voice or many, public prayer is closer to poetry than prose and should, therefore, look more like poetry than prose. If it looks like poetry, it will tend to be spoken accordingly.

Thus, the materials in this book are formatted in short "sense lines" (sometimes called "thought lines" or "breath lines") whereby each line contains enough sense to be understood as a unit even when it is grammatically inseparable from the next. When there is no punctuation mark, the end of the line denotes an almost imperceptible pause, as in the previously quoted collect for Epiphany Sunday (see p. xii):

Toddler Christ

(*Spoken by a worship leader or in unison*)

Toddler Christ, whose light shines out,
not from a palace,
but from a village woman's lap,
shine on us today
through the youngest and the least,
that we may open our treasures
and give them precious gifts
in your name.

If this prayer is spoken in unison, some congregations may need a word of explanation to avoid getting out of step at "today," "treasures," and "gifts."

If you copy items from this book, please preserve their format, even if some unwritten law urges you to cram as much text as possible into a horizontal, two-page spread. If you want to save trees, recycle bulletins or print them on recycled paper!

In the liturgies and worship elements, three typestyles are used: plain, bold, and italics. In prayers and liturgies other than litanies, plain type is used for the worship leader or for the leading voice when there is more than one speaker. Line spaces between sections show how different voices can be assigned. Bold type denotes the responding voice(s) or the whole congregation. Copy or project the whole prayer if the congregation is responding.

In most of the litanies, one voice speaks a repeated cue, called a bidding, to which one or more voices or the whole congregation say a response. Some biddings and responses can also be sung. Because bidding and response are easily learned, litanies are friendly to nonreaders (adult or child), prereaders, and sight-impaired worshipers because it is not essential to print them. The bidding (*in italics*) and response (**in bold**) are spoken responsively by a worship leader and congregation or by two worship leaders, or the bidding and response are the same phrase, spoken and then echoed (e.g., "*Thanks be to God*—**Thanks be to God**"). If you project or print a litany, help nonreaders, prereaders, and sight-impaired worshipers by announcing and practicing the bidding and response immediately before the prayer begins. To add musical enrichment, use the sung responses provided or make up your own. Teach the melody by ear, with or without a printed melody line.

Language and Theology

Grounded in Trinitarian theology, this book offers a variety of ways that the divine mystery can be encountered in public prayer. The whole being of God is addressed as Holy Trinity, wrapped in light; mysterious, hidden, and revealed; God of incomparable love; mother of creation; sovereign love; source of all wisdom; compassionate and faithful; owner and Creator; on the move; in our midst; caregiving; exuberant, life-giving; keeper of the secrets of creation; governor of creation; compassionate, mysterious, and faithful; God of promise and hope; source of loving unity; and God of surpassing peace.

The third person of the Trinity is infrequently addressed at this season of the year but is encountered as Spirit of God, Holy Spirit, and life-changing Spirit.

The second person of the Trinity is encountered as living Christ, Jesus of Nazareth; teacher, friend, Savior, and Lord; welcoming Christ; sovereign leader; Mary's child; faithful Jew; star of hope; energetic Word; active expression of Divinity; Wisdom of God, playful and profound; agent of God's perfection; priest and minister of God; risen Christ; toddler Christ; and radiant Christ, light of the world, whose death, life, and birth are illuminated by the glory of the resurrection, as in the following hymn:

Sing my song backwards from end to beginning,
Friday to Monday, from dying to birth.
Nothing is altered, but hope changes everything:
sing "Resurrection!" and "Peace upon Earth!"

Whisper a hope through the fear in Gethsemane,
horror and emptiness darker than night;
visit the wounds, and the failure of Calvary:
sing "Resurrection!" and bathe them in light.

Gather the bones and the sinews of memory—
healings and parables, laughter and strife,
joy with the outcasts and love for the enemy—
breathe "Resurrection!" and dance them to life.

Stretch out a rainbow from cross to nativity.
Deck out the stable with shepherds and kings,
angels and miracles, glory and poetry—
Sing my song backwards, till all the world sings![2]

BRIAN A. WREN
November 2007

---

2. Brian Wren. Copyright © 1983, 1995 by Hope Publishing Company for the USA, Canada, Australia, and New Zealand, and by Stainer & Bell for all other territories. All rights reserved. Used by permission.

Hymnal Abbreviations

Hymn suggestions in worship services are from a selection of recent denominational hymnals using the acronyms below. The wording varies from hymnal to hymnal. For hymn numbers, consult the first-line index. Many other hymnals have some or all of the hymns suggested.

AHB   *Together in Song: Australian Hymn Book II* (East Melbourne, Vic.: HarperCollinsReligious, 1999)

AMNS   *Hymns Ancient & Modern: New Standard* (Anglican Church, U.K.; Hymns Ancient & Modern Ltd., 1983)

BP   *The Book of Praise* (Canada, Presbyterian Church in Canada, 1997)

CH   *Chalice Hymnal* (Disciples of Christ, U.S.A.; St. Louis: Chalice Press, 1995)

CH4   *Church Hymnary—Fourth Edition* (Church of Scotland, U.K.; Church Hymnary Trust, Norwich: Canterbury Press, 2005)

ELW   *Evangelical Lutheran Worship* (Evangelical Lutheran Church in America; Minneapolis: Augsburg Fortress, 2006)

H82   *The Hymnal 1982: According to the Use of the Episcopal Church* (New York: Church Hymnal Corp., 1985)

NCH   *The New Century Hymnal* (United Church of Christ; Cleveland: Pilgrim Press, 1995)

PH   *The Presbyterian Hymnal* (Presbyterian Church, U.S.A.; Louisville, KY: Westminster/John Knox Press, 1990)

RJS   *Rejoice and Sing* (United Reformed Church, U.K.; Oxford: Oxford University Press, 1991)

UMH   *The United Methodist Hymnal: Book of United Methodist Worship* (Nashville: United Methodist Publishing House, 1989)

VU   *Voices United: The Hymn and Worship Book of the United Church of Canada* (Etobicoke, ON: The United Church Publishing House, 1996)

CHAPTER 1

Liturgies and Worship Elements for Advent in Any Year

The Hanging of the Greens—An Act of Worship for the Beginning of Advent

This intergenerational liturgy places symbolic pieces of evergreen vegetation prominently in the worship space to celebrate God's incarnate love, touched and seen in Jesus of Nazareth. People of all ages and conditions can be involved, some to speak, others to put the objects in place. A worship leader or leaders speak the sections in plain type. All sing the response, printed in boldface, to one of the tunes listed, which are widely known or easily learned. Go through this liturgy with worship leaders beforehand in the worship space so that everyone knows who is doing what, how, and when. The "greens" can be left in place for one or several Sundays. The Christmas Tree section is optional. The United Methodist *Book of Worship* suggested the framework for this liturgy.

> Let us prepare for God's eternal Word,
> touched and seen in Jesus
> by bringing things that we can touch and see
> as signs of God's goodness and love.

Sung Response: **Love that rules the universe**
lived and suffered, died for us:
life abundant, touched and seen,
ever living, ever-green.[1]

BRIAN WREN. POETIC METER: 7.7.7.7. SUITABLE TUNES INCLUDE CANTERBURY, MONKLAND, ORIENTIS PARTIBUS, SAVANNAH, AND SONG 13.

Cedar Wood: A Sign of Majesty

> Listen to this promise from the prophecies of Jeremiah:
>
> > The days are coming, says the Living God,
> > when I shall make a righteous Branch spring from
> >   David's line,
> > a king who will rule wisely,
> > maintaining justice and right in the land.
> >
> > (*Jer. 23:5 REB**)

---

1. Brian Wren. Copyright © 1989 by Hope Publishing Company for the USA, Canada, Australia, and New Zealand, and by Stainer & Bell for all other territories. All rights reserved. Used by permission. This chorus may be reproduced free of charge in The Hanging of the Greens liturgy provided that this copyright notice is printed with it as specified on p. ix above.

Cedar was regarded as a royal tree, signifying immortality.
We place this cedar branch to praise the living Christ
whose love forever rules the universe.

(The cedar branch is set in place. Then all sing the response.)

Holly and Ivy: Signs of Pain and Love

Here are some words of insight from the prophecies of Isaiah:

He had no form or majesty that we should look at him,
nothing in his appearance that we should desire him.
He was despised and rejected by others;
a man of suffering and acquainted with infirmity;
. . . .
But he was wounded for our transgressions,
crushed for our iniquities;
upon him was the punishment that made us whole,
and by his bruises we are healed.   (*Isa. 53:2b–3, 5*)

Ivy has bitter bark and prickly leaves;
its berries are red, the color of blood.
We place holly and ivy
to remember how Jesus endured bitter suffering,
wore a crown of thorns,
and gave his life for us.

(When the holly and ivy are in place, all sing the response.)

An Evergreen Wreath: Sign of Life and Peace

Listen to these words of hope from the prophecies of Isaiah:

The people who walked in darkness have seen a great light;
For a child has been born for us, . . . and he is named:
Wonderful Counselor, Mighty God,
Everlasting Father, Prince of Peace.
His authority shall grow continually, . . . with endless peace,
and justice and righteousness evermore.
                    (*Isa. 9:2a, 6ac, 7abde**)

The green that remains when other leaves fall
shows life undying and hope forever green.
We place this wreath, shaped in a circle,

as a sign of life and hope,
for a circle has no end, and the wreath is ever-green.

(When the wreath is in place, all sing the response.)

The Christmas Tree: Light in Darkness

Listen to these words from the Gospel of John:
Here is good news:

In the beginning was the Word,
and the Word was with God, and the Word was God.
All things came into being through the Word. . . .
What has come into being . . . was life,
and the life was the light of all people.
The light shines in the darkness,
and the darkness did not understand it or overcome it.

The living Christ declares,
I am the light of the world.
Whoever follows me will never walk in darkness
but will have the light of life.

(John 1:1–5 and 8–12*)

(The Christmas tree lights are switched on.)

May this tree remind us of Jesus Christ,
who gives life to the world
and made his executioners' cross into a tree of light.

(All sing the response.)

Advent Hymns by Brian Wren

Hymns are poems of faith, sung or spoken. Worship is enriched when hymns are treated as poems and read aloud in worship. Thus, the hymns in this section can be spoken as poems, sung by soloist(s) or choir, or sung by a congregation. Anyone who legally has this book may speak these poems aloud from it. To access the music and obtain permission to *reproduce* words or music, follow the copyright information on page ix.

Christ Will Come Again[2]

POETIC METER: 5.6.6.6.8.8.8.6.

Christ will come again,
God's justice to complete,
to reap the fields of time
and sift the weeds from wheat:
  then let us passionately care
  for peace and justice here on earth,
and evil's rage restrain with love,
till Christ shall come again.

Christ will come again
and life shall be complete.
The waters from the throne
shall wash the nations' feet:
  then let us passionately care
  for health and wholeness here on earth,
and ease our neighbor's pain with love,
till Christ shall come again.

Christ will come again,
and joy shall be complete
as flames of lightning love
bedeck the judgment seat:
  then let us passionately share
  the whole great gospel here on earth,
until all things attain their end,
when Christ shall come again.

2. Brian Wren. Copyright © 1989 by Hope Publishing Company for the USA, Canada, Australia, and New Zealand, and by Stainer & Bell for all other territories. All rights reserved. Used by permission.

God of Many Names[3]

POETIC METER: 5.5.8.8.D PLUS REFRAIN (PRINTED IN BOLD)

God of many Names,
   gathered into One,
in your glory come and meet us,
Moving, endlessly Becoming.
God of Hovering Wings,
   Womb and Birth of time,
joyfully we sing your praises,
Breath of life in every people—
   Hush, hush, hallelujah, hallelujah!
   Shout, shout, hallelujah, hallelujah!
   Sing, sing, hallelujah, hallelujah!
   Sing, God is love, God is love!

God of Jewish faith,
   Exodus and Law,
in your glory come and meet us,
joy of Miriam and Moses;
   God of Jesus Christ,
   Rabbi of the poor,
joyfully we sing your praises,
crucified, alive for ever—
   Hush, hush, hallelujah, hallelujah!
   Shout, shout, hallelujah, hallelujah!
   Sing, sing, hallelujah, hallelujah!
   Sing, God is love, God is love!

God of wounded hands,
   web and loom of love,
in your glory come and meet us,
Carpenter of new creation;
   God of many Names,
   gathered into One,
joyfully we sing your praises,
Moving, endlessly Becoming—
   Hush, hush, hallelujah, hallelujah!
   Shout, shout, hallelujah, hallelujah!
   Sing, sing, hallelujah, hallelujah!
   Sing, God is love, God is love!

3. Brian Wren. Copyright © 1986 by Hope Publishing Company for the USA, Canada, Australia, and New Zealand, and by Stainer & Bell for all other territories. All rights reserved. Used by permission.

Welcome the Wild One [4]

On John the Baptizer
POETIC METER: 11.10.11.10. DACTYLIC

Welcome the wild one, the desert declaimer,
urgently, awesomely, crying his news:
"Now, listen now! there is One who comes after!
I am unfitted to fasten his shoes."

Camel-hair coated, unkempt and unbending,
living off grasshoppers, honey, and briars,
knee-deep in water, he hails the impending
flame-giving Spirit's enveloping fires.

Hear from the herald the king who's expected:
world-ending wrath is the power he describes,
God's own anointed, outspoken, uncensored,
judging the palace, the priests, and the scribes.

See now the young one who lingers and listens,
standing intent in the buzz of the throng,
waiting in line, on the brink of decisions,
seeking the Spirit that beckons through John.

Gaspingly drenched by the people's baptizer,
drowned in the grief of our groanings and cries,
bowing beneath God's unfettered outsider,
rising envisioned, he opens his eyes.

Welcome God's Love-Child, anointed, invested,
desert-impelled by the Spirit within.
World-making love, shining, tempered and tested,
now is at hand—let salvation begin!

4. Brian Wren. Copyright © 1989 by Hope Publishing Company for the USA, Canada, Australia, and New Zealand, and by Stainer & Bell for all other territories. All rights reserved. Used by permission. Matthew 3:1–17; Mark 1:1–12; Luke 3:1–22.

Who Comes? [5]

POETIC METER: 4.8.6.6.8.6.4.6.8.6.

Who comes? A child,
delivered on a stable floor.
His mewing, newborn cry
  is all that God can say
  of costly, unprotected love
  in Christ, alive today.
Come, singing fire
  of truth, compassion, right,
  and melt our hardened apathy,
  till love is new and bright.

Who comes? A Jew,
declaiming from a prophet's scroll.
His liberating cry
  all that God can say
  of seeking, freeing, saving love
  in Christ, alive today.
Come, singing breeze
  from worlds already new.
  Blow in and out of weary hearts,
  till faith is singing too.

Who comes? A man,
in dying moments on a cross.
His God-forsaken cry
  is all that God can say
  of faithful, never-ending love
  in Christ, alive today.
Come, singing light
  from new creation's dawn,
  where trees of healing deck the streets,
  and joy is newly born.

5. Brian Wren. Copyright © 1986, 1996 by Hope Publishing Company for the USA, Canada, Australia, and New Zealand, and by Stainer & Bell for all other territories. All rights reserved. Used by permission.

Worship Songs for Advent and Christmas

This section contains three worship songs for use in Advent as well as in the Christmas Services of Scripture and Song. If you follow the Revised Common Lectionary (RCL), you will find that the songs echo themes and readings in its three years. The songs can also be used independently of the RCL. Scripture sources are provided. The words and music are copyright © 2000 Praise Partners Publishing (Susan Heafield and Brian Wren) and may be reproduced in worship free of charge on the terms of the copyright notice on page ix.

The source of all three songs is a collection titled *We Can Be Messengers: Worship Songs—Christmas, Before and After*, by Susan Heafield and Brian Wren (book and/or CD). This work, together with its companion volume, *Tell the Good News! Worship Songs—Easter, Before and After*, is distributed by Hope Publishing company—www.hopepublishing.com

The lyrics are followed by Scripture sources and words with music.

Someone Comes!

An Advent/Christmas Song Suitable for RCL Year A

(Add a verse a week, or make a selection. Sing the refrain at the beginning and after each verse.)

Refrain: **Someone comes to make things right,
tomorrow, today, tonight.
Jesus comes to make things right,
tomorrow, today, tonight.**

Angry people will shake hands,
they won't learn war any more.
Melt your guns and turn them into plows,
and don't learn war any more.

(Refrain)

Hungry people will be fed,
they won't be hurt any more.
See the children playing in the street?
They won't be hurt any more.

(Refrain)

Hurting people will be healed,
they won't be afraid any more.

No-one's dirty or unclean,
so don't be afraid any more.

(*Refrain*)

Someone's coming, coming soon,
we won't be alone any more.
God is with us, all the time.
We won't be alone any more.

(*Refrain*)

Hold the Christ Child in your arms
and sing for joy evermore.
Light is shining in the night,
so sing for joy evermore!

(*Refrain*)

Great Holy One

An Advent/Christmas Song Suitable for RCL Year B

(Add a verse a week or make a selection. Suggestion: Each Sunday, read the new verse to the congregation before it is sung. Sundays 1–4: Sing refrain after each verse, and bridge plus refrain after the new verse. Sunday 5: Use bridge plus refrain after verses 3 and 5.)

Refrain: **Great, Holy One,**
spreading time and space,
show us who you are
in a human face.

Bridge: Hide and seek:
learn to trust,
no one's really ever lost.
Hide and seek:
when we're found,
we'll be safe on holy ground.

Hidden One, how can we meet you,
when our world is filled with pain
and our praying is in vain?
If we knock and get no answer,
and we cannot cope,
help us still to hope.

(*Refrain*)

Awesome One, where can we find you?
"In the wisdom of a child,
in opponents reconciled.
When you meet with sudden kindness,
find my holy place
in your neighbor's face."

(*Refrain*)

Seeking One, how will you meet us?
"In the person who resists
hate and greed, and then persists;
when my people work together,
righting ancient wrongs,
singing peaceful songs."

(*Refrain*)

Loving One, how have you found us?
"Through the people that I choose,
through the story of the Jews:
Abraham and Ruth and Moses,
Martha, Peter, Paul—
Jesus, above all."

(*Refrain*)

Living One, how will you lead us?
"Not by scheming, not by stealth,
not with glamour, power, and wealth,
but through Jesus, teacher, healer,
in a manger born,
now on Christmas morn.

(*Refrain*)

Rejoice, Give Thanks!

An Advent/Christmas Song Suitable for RCL Year C

(Add a verse a week, or make a selection.)

Turn on the porch light,
dazzle the dark night.
God is coming soon.
God is coming soon
through someone, somehow,
next year, here and now,
midnight, morning, noon.

So don't be tempted or distracted
by the daily grind,
and the peace of God in Jesus Christ
will guard our heart and mind.

Just like a snowplow,
scraping a road now,
prophets clear the way.
Prophets clear away
our shame and sadness,
blame and busyness,
calling us to pray.
 In love's great furnace we'll be burnished,
 rescued and refined,
 and the peace of God in Jesus Christ
 will guard our heart and mind.

Here is a newsbreak
healing our heartache:
Christ will bring us home!
Christ will bring us home,
where no one's outcast,
and we'll have at last
freedom and shalom.
 In hope we're living, let thanksgiving
 all our fears unwind,
 and the peace of God in Jesus Christ
 will guard our heart and mind.

Born in a stable,
straw for a cradle,
now the baby cries,
and the baby's cries
bring down the tyrant,
break the arrogant,
sifting truth from lies.
 Rejoice! The hungry shall have plenty,
 all who seek will find,
 and the peace of God in Jesus Christ
 will guard our heart and mind.

Thousands of angels
stand in the heavens,
singing, "Christ is born!
Jesus Christ is born,

and death is outdone,
evil overcome.
Never be forlorn!"
   Rejoice, give thanks, for God is near us,
   loving, true, and kind,
   and the peace of God in Jesus Christ
   will guard our heart and mind.

Scripture Sources for "Someone Comes!"

First Sunday in Advent—Angry People Will Shake Hands

RCL READINGS: ISAIAH 2:1–5; PSALM 122; ROMANS 13: 11–14; MATTHEW 24:36–44

Isaiah 2:1–5 (Peace: people shall come to God, who will arbitrate; swords into plowshares; not learn war any more); Matthew 24:36–44 (Keep awake; you don't know how or when your Lord is coming). See also Psalm 122 and Romans 13:11–14.

Second Sunday in Advent—Hungry People Will Be Fed

RCL READINGS: ISAIAH 11:1–10; PSALM 72:1–7, 18–19; ROMANS 15:4–13; MATTHEW 3:1–12

Isaiah 11:1–10 (Justice for all, especially the poor. Equity, the shoot from the stump—new life from old roots—the Spirit of God will rest on him; by his words he will bring justice for the weak); Matthew 3:1–12 (John the Baptizer: "I baptize with water; the one who comes after is mightier than I, and will baptize with Holy Spirit and fire. Bear fruits worthy of repentance"). See also Psalm 72:1–7, 18–19 (a king bringing justice) and Romans 15:4–13.

Third Sunday in Advent—Hurting People Will Be Healed

RCL READINGS: ISAIAH 35: 1–10; PSALM 146:5–10 OR LUKE 1:47–55; JAMES 5:7–10; MATTHEW 11:2–11

Isaiah 35:1–10 (Healing: water in the desert, new life from dry land; the blind shall see, the deaf hear, the lame walk. God will make a holy way); Matthew 11:2–11 (John the Baptizer asks Jesus, "Are you the one?" Jesus replies, "The blind see, deaf hear, lame walk, lepers are cleansed. Blessed is the one who takes no offense at me." The healing of the most vulnerable is a sign of Christ among us).

Fourth Sunday in Advent —Someone's Coming, Coming Soon

RCL READINGS: ISAIAH 7:10–16; PSALM 80:1–7, 17–19; ROMANS 1:1–7; MATTHEW 1:18–25

Isaiah 7:10–16 (God gives a sign that Judah will be delivered from an invading army: a pregnant young woman will bear a child and call him Immanuel ["With-Us-God"]. When he's old enough to "refuse evil and choose good" [= choosing kinds of food when weaned?], danger will be past. This is a sign of God with us); Matthew 1:18–25 (Joseph accepts Mary's pregnancy; will name her son Jesus [Yeshua = Joshua = Liberator], God with us in person). See also Psalm 80:1–7, 17–19 and Romans 1:1–7.

Christmas Eve/Day—Hold the Christ Child in Your Arms

RCL READINGS: ISAIAH 9:2–7; PSALM 96; TITUS 2:11–14; LUKE 2:1–14 (15–20)

Isaiah 9:2–7 (The people who walked in darkness have seen great light. A child with authority will bring peace with justice; causes great joy); Luke 2:1–20 (the birth of Jesus; on a dark night angels bring light and good news of great joy). See also Psalm 96 and Titus 2:11–14

Scripture Sources for "Great Holy One"

First Sunday in Advent—Hidden One, How Can We Meet You?

RCL READINGS: ISAIAH 64:1–9; PSALM 80:1–7, 17–19; 1 CORINTHIANS 1:3–9; MARK 13:24–37

Isaiah 64:1–9 (God is hidden—"O that you would rend the heavens and come down"). See also Psalm 80:1–7, 17–19 ("How long will you be angry with your people's prayers"; "we knock and get no answer").

Second Sunday in Advent—Awesome One, Where Can We Find You?

RCL READINGS: ISAIAH 40:1–11; PSALM 85:1–2, 8–13; 2 PETER 3:8–15A; MARK 1:1–8

Psalm 85:8–13 (righteousness [= justice] and peace); Mark 1:1–8 ("in a human face"); Isaiah 11:6 (a little child shall lead them); and Matthew 25:31–46 (Christ in the neighbor).

Third Sunday in Advent—Seeking One, How Will You Meet Us?

RCL READINGS: ISAIAH 61:1–4, 8–11; PSALM 126 OR LUKE 1:47–55; 1 THESSALONIANS 5:16–24;
JOHN 1:6–8, 19–28

Isaiah 61:1–4 (Resisting hate and greed; righting ancient wrongs); so also Luke 1:47–55. For the bridge passage, see 1 Thessalonians 5:16–24 (Learn to trust: God is faithful.)

Fourth Sunday in Advent—Loving One, How Have You Found Us?

RCL READINGS: 2 SAMUEL 7:1–11, 16; LUKE 1:47–55 OR PSALM 89:1–4, 19–26; ROMANS 16:25–27;
LUKE 1:26–38

Second Samuel 7:1–11, 16 (The story of the Jews); so also Luke 1:47–55; Romans 16:25–27 (God's revelation); Luke 1:26–38 (Jesus, born of Mary). See also Genesis 12:1–9; Exodus 2–4; Ruth; Luke 10:38–42; John 11:17–27.

Christmas Eve/Day—Living One, How Will You Lead Us?

RCL READINGS: ISAIAH 9:2–7; PSALM 96; TITUS 2:11–14; LUKE 2:1–14 (15–20)

For "Not by scheming, stealth, glamour, power, and wealth," see Luke 2:1–14 and, for example, Luke 9:23–25, 46–48, 57–58 and 22:24–27.

Scripture Sources for "Rejoice! Give Thanks!"

First Sunday in Advent—Turn on the Porch Light

RCL READINGS: JEREMIAH 33:14–16; PSALM 25:1–10; 1 THESSALONIANS 3:9–13; LUKE 21:25–36

Luke 21:25–36 (Be alert, v. 36) and 1 Thessalonians 3:13. The last two lines of the refrain are based on Philippians 4:4–7 (see Third Sunday in Advent). See also Psalm 25:1–10 (Trust in God).

Second Sunday in Advent—Just Like a Snowplow

RCL READINGS: MALACHI 3:1–4; LUKE 1:68–79; PHILIPPIANS 1:3–11; LUKE 3:1–6

Malachi 3:1–4 (in love's great furnace/prophets clear away . . .), Luke 1:68–79 (John the Baptizer will clear the way for Christ), and Luke 3:1–6 (ditto).

Third Sunday in Advent—Here Is a Newsbreak

RCL READINGS: ZEPHANIAH 3:14–20; ISAIAH 12:2–6; PHILIPPIANS 4:4–7; LUKE 3:7–18

Zephaniah 3:14–20 ("I will bring you home") and Isaiah 12:2–6 (In hope we are living).

Fourth Sunday in Advent—Born in a Stable

RCL READINGS: MICAH 5:2–5A; LUKE 1:47–55 OR PSALM 80:1–7; HEBREWS 10:5–10; LUKE 1:39–45 (46–55)

Micah 5:2–5a (from Bethlehem comes a peace bringer) and Luke 1:47–55 (a baby's cries bring down the tyrant and break the arrogant).

Christmas Eve/Day—Thousands of Angels

RCL READINGS: ISAIAH 9:2–7; PSALM 96; TITUS 2:11–14; LUKE 2:1–14 (15–20)

Titus 2:11–14 (God is near us) and Luke 2:1–20 (the angel song).

"Someone Comes!"—Music of Stanzas 1–3. Stanzas 4–5 are musically identical.

Someone Comes!

Words by Brian Wren

Music by Susan Heafield

Words: Brian Wren; Music: Susan Heafield.
Copyright © 2000 Praise Partners Publishing. All Rights Reserved.

Great Holy One

Words by Brian Wren   Music by Susan Heafield

Refrain

Great Ho - ly One, spread-ing time and space,

show us who you are in a hu - man face.

Hid - den one, _____ how can we find _ you, when our
Awe - some one, _____ how shall we meet you? "In the
Seek - ing one, _____ how will you meet us? "In the

world is filled with pain, and our pray - ing is in vain? _
wis - dom of a child in op - po - nents re - con - ciled?
per - son who re - sists, hate and greed and then per - sists; _

Great Ho - ly One,   spread-ing time and space,

show us who You are   in a hu - man face.

Lov - ing one, _____ how have you found us? "Through the
Liv - ing one, _____ how will you lead us? "Not by

peo - ple that I choose, through the stor - y of the Jews:
schem-ing or by stealth, not with glam-our, power, and wealth,

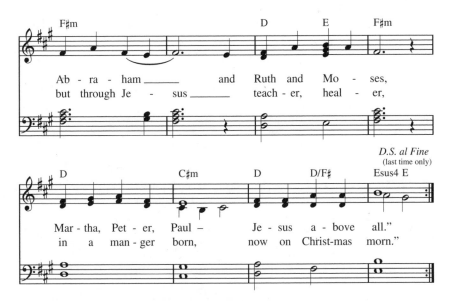

Ab - ra - ham _____ and Ruth and Mo - ses,
but through Je - sus _____ teach - er, heal - er,

D.S. al Fine
(last time only)

Mar - tha, Pet - er, Paul — Je - sus a - bove all."
in a man - ger born, now on Christ-mas morn."

Words: Brian Wren; Music: Susan Heafield.
Copyright © 2000 Praise Partners Publishing. All Rights Reserved.

"Rejoice! Give Thanks"—Music of Stanzas 1–3. Stanzas 4–5 are musically identical.

Rejoice, Give Thanks

Words by Brian Wren

Music by Susan Heafield

Re - joice, give thanks for God is near us, lov - ing, true, and kind, ___ and the peace of God in Je - sus ___ Christ will guard our heart and mind.

Turn on the porch light, daz - zle the dark night. God is com - ing soon.
Just like a snow-plow, scrap-ing a road now, proph-ets clear the way.
Here is a news-break heal - ing our heart-ache; Christ will bring us home!

God is com - ing soon through some - one, some - how,
Proph-ets clear a - way our ___ shame and sad - ness,
Christ will bring us home, where no one's out - cast,

Words: Brian Wren; Music: Susan Heafield.
Copyright © 2000 Praise Partners Publishing. All Rights Reserved.

Pastoral and Meditative Prayers for Advent

Beginning and End

A Pastoral Prayer

(Spoken by a worship leader; use this prayer in whole or in part. Add particular prayer concerns as appropriate.)

Mysterious God, hidden and revealed,
first and last, beginning and end,
we worship and adore you.

With effortless ease
you name and hold in mind
every life, every life form, and every human being.

You create us and give us breath.
You delight in the work of your hands.
You know us and call us by name,
and nothing can separate us from your love.

And so we have confidence to admit
that we belong to a race, the human race,
that hides from you,
refuses and resists your love,
avoids your gaze,
and seeks satisfaction in lesser gods.

We confess our own part
in denying that we belong to you,
by hiding or running away,
giving ourselves to other powers,
and resisting your love.

We are sorry,
for wrongdoing that ensnares us
and wrongdoing that we have chosen.

Forgive us and set us free.
Turn us back to you.
Turn us toward each other in love.

Loving God, beginning and end,
we thank you and praise you
for ancestors, known and unknown,
held in memory, or hidden in time,
and for the forms of life
from which we have descended
and which have left their mark
in our body and brain.

We praise you
for people with whom we are connected—
in this congregation,
at home or work,
through kinship and friendship
and through TV, books, and other media.
Thank you for all who shape us for good
and make us what we are.
  (We pray especially for . . . .)

We pray for all living things.
Protect endangered species.
Preserve the web of life
on which our life depends.
In our care for the earth,
forestall the mistakes
of people and leaders
and deflect our dangerous decisions.

We pray for earth's creatures, now and in the future,
and for the human generations that follow us,
especially for those who descend from us
by kinship or by choice.
Give them a good earth
with ample food, pure air,
and clean water.
Give them peace and hope,
and people to love.

Mysterious God, beginning and end,
first and last,
hidden and revealed,
all glory and honor are yours,
now and for ever. Amen.

Giver of Hope

A Pastoral Prayer

(*Spoken by a worship leader; use it in whole or in part. Add particular prayer concerns as appropriate.*)

Spirit of God,
you open doors that are locked,
break the shackles of slavery,
erode the pyramids of domination,
and tumble tyrants from their thrones.

You give us life
and whisper in our hearts,
"You are God's beloved child,
and always will be."

Deep in every human heart
you plant a seed of promise,
a glimmer of expectation,
and a spark of hope.

And because you give us breath,
we praise you.

Do not give up on us
when we let go of hope,
surrender to disappointment,
drift into aimlessness,
or sink into gloom and despair.

Stir us, again and again,
to dream of new possibilities,
and energize each other
with new expectations.

Hear our prayer
for all who wait in hope
for a smile, a handshake, and a welcome;
and for all who long to find
joy beyond sorrow,
healing beyond hurt,
peace beyond conflict,
and dawn after dark night,

Resurrect the hopes
of people bruised and beaten.
Fan into flame the spark of hope
in caregivers racked with tiredness,
prisoners locked in isolation,
and people held captive
by illness and addiction.

Breathe and blow through this congregation
and kindle your gifts
of patience, kindness, humility,
fidelity, gentleness, and self-control.
Revive in us now
the freedom to give and receive,
to make mistakes and start again
to forgive and accept forgiveness.

Energize the worldwide church.
Strengthen those who are persecuted for their faith.
Give courage to women, children, and men
who day by day struggle to survive.

Hold us all in communion,
that through differences of culture and conviction,
we may hear the world say,
"These Christians love each other.
This is something new."

To you, most humble, most wise,
yet ever untamable Spirit,
with the Word made flesh
and the Source of all things,
Holy Three, Holy One,
be glory and honor,
worship and praise,
now and for ever. Amen.

Mothering God

A Pastoral Prayer

(*Spoken by a worship leader; use it in whole or in part. Add particular prayer concerns as appropriate.*)

Holy God, Mother of creation,
conceiving time and space
and bringing life to birth,
we praise you.

Distinct from all your creatures
yet intimately connected,
you watch over us, and all the human race.
You know us through and through,
call us by name,
and fill us with dignity and worth.

And although we ignore your warnings,
run from your embrace,
and turn our back on your kindness,
nothing can separate us from your love.

Show us your passion for our good
and your compassion for all.
If we are trapped and imprisoned, set us free.
If we have broken your commandments, forgive us
and set us on a new course.
If we have strayed and lost our way,
Bring us home.

Created as your children,
you call us into a new family
in Jesus Christ,
making us sisters and brothers to each other.
Therefore, at all times and in all places
we praise you
as we pray for the members of Christ's body
here, and throughout the world.

Mothering God, giver of birth and the power to give birth,
hear our particular prayers.

Comfort those who have lost a child—
in youth and adulthood, childhood or infancy,

by miscarriage or stillbirth.
Give them friends to recognize their loss,
rituals of loss and hope,
and the unscheduled healing of your Spirit.

Give wisdom and patience
to all who long to have children,
and who wait in hope
for conception, birth, or adoption;
and guide all parents
through the maze of discipline and love.

Give life and hope to your church
and to cities and towns,
neighborhoods and nations
that long for new vision and new birth.

Rekindle among us
the good news that in Jesus Christ
the desert can blossom,
the lost can be found,
and young and old can be reborn.
Grow in our hearts
the hope of ultimate newness
before and after death
and in your new creation.

To you, Living God, our Mother, Father, Sovereign, and
    Friend,
we give ourselves, as Christ's body,
in thanksgiving and praise. Amen.

God of Incomparable Love

A Meditative Prayer on the Preaching of John the Baptizer

(*Spoken by a worship leader; use it in whole or in part. Add particular prayer concerns as appropriate.*)

God of incomparable love,
thank you for the gift of life,
for the gift of this day,
and for everyone who prepared the way
for the coming of Jesus Christ.

Thank you for John the Baptizer,
who was so committed to you
that he gave himself utterly to your Word,
living rough in the desert,
in awe of your holiness,
expecting your imminent coming,
risking and giving his life.

We wonder why John was convinced
that your Messiah would come
to separate good from bad,
fruitful from fruitless,
wheat from chaff,
with overwhelming violence,
and to burn dead lives and dead wood
in unquenchable fire?

And yet, though we know with hindsight
that Jesus doesn't work that way,
perhaps there is a part of us
that wishes John was right.

For if we are haunted by terror,
silenced by abuse and violation,
or afraid of violent crime,
it seems such a comforting thought
that your Chosen One on earth
will come with fire
to end our fears,
using ultimate force
that is righteous and good.

So perhaps if Jesus came on our block,
we would say in our hearts,
"Where is your gun for protection?
Is all you can bring us
a body unarmed, a healing touch,
and a hopeful word?"

And yet, we are bound to thank you
that Jesus came unprotected and unarmed,
announcing good news to the poor,
living your healing peace,
and standing among us, risen from the dead,
with wounds of undying love.

Therefore, in the Spirit of Jesus
we pray for this violent world.
Heal the victims of violence and abuse.
Bring abusers and violators to account
and to repentance.
Comfort those who are wounded within
by violence they witness
or violence they use against others.
Make officers of law enforcement
patient, trustworthy, and wise.
Save children and youth from bullying and intimidation.
Tame our thirst for revenge,
and water the seeds of mercy
in our government, lawcourts, and prisons,
and in us.

Help us, like John the Baptizer,
to act on your truth as we hear it.
Redeem our mistakes and shortcomings,
and make us reliable witnesses
to the One who came after John,
who comes today, and will come again,
Jesus, your Word and Presence,
in whose name we pray.

CHAPTER 2

Advent Liturgies and Worship Elements

(YEAR A)

Liturgies for Placing an Advent Candle Ring and Lighting the Advent and Christ Candles

The Advent and Christ candles liturgies draw on the RCL Year A readings from Isaiah 2:1–5; 11:1–10; 35:1–10; and 7:10–16.

Use five separate candlesticks or use a prepared ring with holders for the first four candles at its "compass points" on the rim and a fifth holder in the middle. Have the candles far enough apart to minimize burn risk to the candle lighters.

People of all ages and conditions can be involved—some to speak, others to light the candle(s). Deal with Scripture sources as suggested on page xii.

A worship leader or leaders speak the sections in plain type. The leaders together or the whole congregation say the responses printed in bold. If possible, practice with worship leaders beforehand in the worship space so that everyone knows who is doing what, how, and when. Light the first candle on the first Sunday. Thereafter, relight the previous candles as this liturgy begins so that attention then focuses on the new candle being lit that day.

First Sunday in Advent: Placing an Advent Candle Ring and Lighting the First Advent Candle

We shall light the Advent candles/place this candle ring,
praying that our preparation for Christmas may help us
to look outward in love,
and to look forward in hope.
**Risen Christ, Light of the world,
shine in our lives
and shine among us now.**

(If a candle ring is used, set it in place.)

Let us pray that waiting for Christmas may show us
how to be patient when things take time,
how to live for Christ day by day,
and how to wait for promises not yet fulfilled.
**Risen Christ, Light of the world,
shine in our lives
and shine among us now.**

In Isaiah, chapter 2, the prophet declares that in days to come
God will judge between the nations,
and arbitrate for many peoples.

(Light the first candle.)

> We light this candle because we refuse to let go of Isaiah's hope
> that swords can be beaten into plowshares,
> and spears into pruning hooks,
> and that nation shall not lift up sword against nation,
> neither shall they learn war any more.   *(Isa. 2:4)*
> **Risen Christ, Light of the world,**
> **shine in our lives**
> **and shine among us now.**

Second Sunday in Advent: Lighting the Second Advent Candle

(Begin with the first candle relit.)

> In Isaiah 11:9, the prophet declares,
>> They will not hurt or destroy on all my holy mountain;
>> for the earth shall be full of the knowledge of God,
>> as the waters cover the sea.
> We light this candle as a sign of hope
> that truth will prevail, and justice be done,
> for all people.

(Light the second candle.)

> As we pray and work
> for truth, compassion, and justice, near and far—
> **Risen Christ, Light of the world,**
> **shine in our lives**
> **and shine among us now.**

Third Sunday in Advent: Lighting the Third Advent Candle

(Begin with the previous candles relit.)

> In Isaiah 35:5–6, the prophet declares that when God comes
>> among us,
> the deaf shall hear, the blind shall see,
> and the tongue of the speechless shall sing for joy.
> We light this candle as a sign of our hope
> that God's love in Christ brings healing to us,
> and to the whole world.

(Light the third candle.)

> As we witness to the power of healing love,
> in ourselves and in others—

Risen Christ, Light of the world,
shine in our lives
and shine among us now.

Fourth Sunday in Advent: Lighting the Fourth Advent Candle

(*Begin with the previous candles relit.*)

The prophet Isaiah declares,
"A young woman is with child,
and shall bear a son, and shall name him Immanuel
[which means: God-With-Us.]."
The risen Christ declares,
"I am with you always, to the end of the age."
(*Isa. 7:14 and Matt. 28:20*)
We light this candle as a sign of God's presence in Christ,
now and always.

(*Light the fourth candle.*)

That we may trust that God is with us
and live in the light of Christ's coming—
**Risen Christ, Light of the world,
shine in our lives
and shine among us now.**

Christmas Eve or Christmas Day: Lighting the Christ Candle

(*Begin with the previous candles relit.*)

Here is good news of great joy, for all people:
God has rescued us from the domain of darkness,
and brought us into the realm of Christ,
in whom our release is secured,
and our sins are forgiven.
The light shines in the darkness,
and the darkness has never captured it.
(*Luke 2:10; Col. 1:13–14; John 1:5*)

(*Light the Christ candle.*)

Let us pray that we may know the warmth and brightness of
Jesus Christ,
and show Christ's love to the world.

**Risen Christ, Light of the world,
shine in our lives
and shine among us now.
Hallelujah! Amen!**

Worship Elements for Particular Sundays

First Sunday in Advent

RCL READINGS: ISAIAH 2:1–5; PSALM 122; ROMANS 13:11–14; MATTHEW 24:36–44

I Rejoiced

A Responsive Call to Worship Drawn from Psalm 122

(Spoken responsively by two voices or by worship leader[s] and congregation. The responding or congregation voice is in bold.)

I rejoiced when people said to me:
"Let us go to the house of God!"
And now, Jerusalem,
we stand within your gates.

All the tribes assemble here
giving thanks to the Holy Name.
Peace be within your walls
and security within your towers.

For the sake of my relatives and friends
I will say, "Peace be within you!"
For the sake of the Holy Name
I will seek your good.

Keeper of the Secrets

A Collect Responding to the Gospel Reading on the First Sunday in Advent in RCL Years A and B

(Spoken by a worship leader or in unison)

Gracious God,
keeper of the secrets of creation,
visit us through the cry of need,
the unforeseen stranger,
and the unexpected guest,
that we may be ready for the coming of Christ
in the midst of life,
at the end of life,
and at the end of time.
Amen.

God of Mercy, God of Peace

Petition and Intercession in Response to the Old Testament Reading from Isaiah 2:1–5 (This is also suitable for the second Sunday in Advent in Year A, as a response to Isaiah 11:1–10.)

*(Spoken responsively by two voices or by worship leader[s] and congregation. The responding or congregation voice is in bold. If the prayer is not printed or projected, briefly teach and practice the bidding and response: "God of mercy, God of peace, **hear our prayer**.")*

Holy and loving God,
your will is that no-one shall hurt or destroy,
yet your world is filled with violence and strife;
we cry out to you in longing and hope:

That we may pray humbly,
longing to see as you see,
and love as you love,
God of mercy, God of peace,
hear our prayer.

For all who learn war
as they practice the care of weapons
and the application of deadly force,
God of mercy, God of peace,
hear our prayer.

For all whom we currently name
as defenders, allies, and enemies—
and for all who name us as their enemies,
God of mercy, God of peace,
hear our prayer.

For children, women, and men
whose bodies become statistics,
or who are regarded as not worth counting,
God of mercy, God of peace,
hear our prayer.

For all whose lives are torn apart
by death, destruction,
and wounds of body and mind,
God of mercy, God of peace,
hear our prayer.

For all who are scarred by the trauma of battle,
who carry unbearable knowledge
and memories they cannot share,
God of mercy, God of peace,
hear our prayer.

For all, including ourselves,
who are swayed, excited, or ruled
by the drumbeats of anger,
the thirst for revenge,
and the seductive appeal of force,
God of mercy, God of peace,
hear our prayer.

In the name of Jesus Christ
who refused to hurt or destroy,
God of mercy, God of peace,
hear our prayer.
Amen.

Advent Hope

An Affirmation of Faith Based on Readings for the First Sunday in Advent in All Three Years of the RCL

(Spoken responsively by two voices or by worship leader[s] and congregation. The responding or congregation voice is in bold.)

Let us affirm our hope in Christ,
who came, who comes,
and who is to come:

When violence reigns,
and war seems never-ending,
Christ is our hope,
born among us,
crucified and risen.

When despair lies in wait
and life loses meaning,
Christ is our hope,
born among us,
crucified and risen.

When people claim to know
what God alone knows,
and say the end is near,
Christ is our hope,
born among us,
crucified and risen.

When life on earth is extinguished
this year, next year,
or in a hundred million years,
Christ is our hope,
born among us,
crucified and risen.

In sorrow and joy,
today and tomorrow,
in life and in death,
Christ is our hope,
born among us,
crucified and risen.

Thanks be to God! Amen.

Second Sunday in Advent

RCL READINGS: ISAIAH 11:1–10; PSALM 72:1–7, 18–19; ROMANS 15:4–13; MATTHEW 3:1–12

Christ Comes!

A Verse for Meditation

"Christ comes!—
In the word on the street
      and the word that forgives,
      Christ comes.
At the end of the day,
at the ultimate end,
Christ Jesus lives and leads.
      God be praised!"[1]

---

1. Verse from the hymn "Christ Leads!" by Brian Wren. Copyright © 2001 by Hope Publishing Company for the USA, Canada, Australia, and New Zealand and Stainer & Bell Limited for all other territories. All rights reserved. Reprinted by permission.

In the Name of Christ, Welcome

A Call to Worship or Invitation to Greet Each Other in Christ's Peace, Based on Romans 15:7–12

(Spoken by a worship leader or leaders)

In the name of Christ, welcome—
from every orientation, location, color, and class—
old and young, female and male, Gentile and Jew—
in the name of Christ, welcome!
Give thanks that Jesus the Jew
became a servant to his people
to confirm the ancient promise
that the Gentiles would glorify God.
We are fruits of Christ's labor,
gathered by God's grace.
Therefore, let us welcome one another,
just as Christ has welcomed us,
for the glory of God.

Come Together, Worship God

A Responsive Call to Worship Echoing the Old Testament and Gospel Readings

(Spoken by a worship leader or responsively by two voices or by worship leader[s] and congregation. The responding or congregation voice is printed in bold.)

Come together, worship God, and dare to hope:
The One who comes
will not judge by appearances,
but will defend the poor with justice
and decide with equity for the meek of the earth.

Come together, worship God,
and dare to believe the promise:
Christ will baptize us with the Holy Spirit,
and with fire.

Come together, worship God,
and dare to respond to the call:
"Repent, and bear fruit worthy of repentance,
for the reign of God is near!'

Blessed be the Holy Name, the God of Israel,
who alone does wonderful things!
May the earth be filled with the knowledge of God
as the waters cover the sea!
Amen, and amen!

Living God, Governor of Creation

A Prayer for Public Servants, Based on Psalm 72

(Spoken by a worship leader)

Living God, Governor of Creation,
hear our prayer
for public servants
and elected leaders.
(and especially today for _____—add *names* and/or
   categories)

Fill them with your Spirit
to judge rightly,
to defend the cause of the poor,
to show mercy to the needy and the weak,
and to deliver us from oppression and violence.

Make them like rain that falls on the mown grass,
like showers that water the earth,
and make righteousness flourish in their days,
through the world's most public servant,
Jesus Christ, to whom be glory and praise. Amen.

By Whose Inspiration

A Collect for Illumination from Romans 15:4–7

(Spoken by a worship leader or in unison)

Spirit of God
by whose inspiration the records of faith were written,
breathe through the speaking of Scripture
that we may have joy and peace in believing,
and abound in hope
through Jesus Christ.
Amen.

Source of Loving Unity

A Trinitarian Collect from Romans 15:4–7

(Spoken by a worship leader or in unison)

Holy God, Three in One,
Source of loving unity,
clothe us with your Spirit
that we may welcome each other
as Christ has welcomed us,
live in harmony together,
and with one voice
give you glory and praise,
through Jesus Christ. Amen.

Friends, Go in Peace

A Blessing from Romans 15:5, 13

(Spoken by a worship leader or leaders)

Friends, go in peace.
Be steadfast in faith.
Live in harmony with one another.
And may the God of hope fill you
with all joy and peace in believing,
so that you may abound in hope
by the power of the Holy Spirit. Amen.

Third Sunday in Advent

RCL READINGS: ISAIAH 35:1–10; PSALM 146:5–10; LUKE 1:47–55 (OPTIONAL); JAMES 5:7–10;
MATTHEW 11:2–11

Happy Are Those

A Call to Worship from Psalm 146, Drawing on Verses 1–4 and 5ff.

(Spoken by a worship leader or leaders, or by worship leader[s] and congregation. The responding or congregation voice is printed in bold.)

Happy are those whose help is the God of Israel,
who made heaven and earth,
the sea, and everything in it!
who keeps faith for ever,
secures justice for the oppressed,
gives food to the hungry
and sets captives free.

We will not rely on rulers,
on human schemes and plans.
**Our help is the Living God,
maker of heaven and earth,
the sea, and everything in it!**

Bring Hopes and Longings

A Call to Worship Echoing Isaiah 35:1–10

(Spoken by one worship leader or by three. If feasible, project appropriate images while these words are spoken.)

A Come. Worship God.
Bring hopes and longings, joy and sadness,
everything you are.

B Come. Worship God together.
Step into God's new world
and taste the poetry of promise:

C The desert shall blossom abundantly,
Burning sand shall become a pool,
and the thirsty ground springs of water.

ABC together The eyes of the blind shall be opened,
and the ears of the deaf unstopped;
The lame shall leap like a deer,
and the tongue of the speechless sing for joy.

A Waters shall break forth in the wilderness,
and streams in the desert;

B A highway shall be there.
It shall be called the Holy Way
and the redeemed shall walk there.

C Everlasting joy shall be upon their heads;
and sorrow and sighing shall flee away.

ABC together Come! Enter God's future.
Step into hope
and worship God.

Come Together, People of God

A Call to Worship or Discipleship for the Third Sunday in Advent Years A and B, Echoing Luke 1:47–55.

(Spoken by a worship leader or leaders as a straightforward invitation omitting the bracketed lines or as a dialogue including them.)

Come together, people of God.
Pray, praise, and listen
to familiar words of revolutionary change.
(Revolutionary? I'm not sure I want to hear this.)
"The Living God does great things for us,
and Holy is her Name.
(Amen! So far, so good!)
She tumbles the mighty,
raises the humble,
scatters the schemers,
feeds the hungry
and dismisses the overfed."
(Wait a moment. Is this in the Bible?
It is? Are you serious, God?)
Come together, people of God.
Pray, praise, and listen
to familiar words of revolutionary change.
(So who's going to do all this? A baby? *Jesus Christ!!*)
"My soul glorifies the living God,
and my spirit rejoices in God my Savior."
(That's what Mary said—A baby, Jesus Christ.)
Come together, people of God
in hope of revolutionary change
(OK. Here I am. Change me!)
for us and the world around us.
Amen.

The People We Avoid

A Meditative Prayer Responding to the Gospel Reading, Especially Matthew 11:3–5

(Spoken by a worship leader or leaders)

Living Christ,
do you want us to love
the people we avoid
with embarrassment, guilt,

anxiety, anger,
revulsion, or disgust?

Will we be shocked and offended
if you embrace them
and bring them to your table?
And are you expecting us
to do the same?

Are you the One who is to come,
or shall we look for another?
Amen.

Fourth Sunday in Advent

RCL READINGS: ISAIAH 7:10–16; PSALM 80:1–7, 17–19; ROMANS 1:1–7; MATTHEW 1:18–25

Claim the Hope That Calls Us

An Affirmation of Faith or Call to Worship Drawn from Psalm 46
and Isaiah 43:1–2, Preparing for or Responding to the Gospel
Reading

*(Spoken responsively by two voices or by worship leader[s] and congregation. The responding
or congregation voice is printed in bold.)*

Let us worship God and claim the hope that calls us:

God is our refuge and strength,
a very present help in trouble.
Therefore, we will not be terrified,
though the earth should open up in front of us,
though the mountains shake in the heart of the sea.
The Holy Name is with us.
The God of Abraham is our refuge.

The Holy Name declares:
"Do not be afraid. I am with you.
I have called you by name. You are mine.
When you pass through the waters, I will be with you;
and through the rivers, they shall not overwhelm you."
The Holy Name is with us.
The God of Sarah is our refuge.

Weaver of Time and Space

An Advent Call to Worship

(Spoken by a worship leader or by a worship leader and congregation. The congregation voice is printed in bold.)

> Listen. Here is good news.
> The Living God, Weaver of time and space,
> far beyond us, nearer than body and bone,
> is joining us in person,
> growing in a mother's womb,
> delivered in the labor of birth,
> washed and clothed,
> cradled, nursed, and fed.
> **This is a wonder and a mystery.**
> **This is good news of great joy.**
> **Thank God! Thank God!**

Child of a Human Mother

A Prayer of Praise and Adoration in Response to the Gospel Reading

(Spoken by a worship leader or in unison)

> Compassionate Creator,
> conceiving and giving birth to all things,
> we praise and adore you
> for coming to us in the flesh
> as the child of a human mother,
> Emmanuel, God with us.
> Amen.

Call and Prepare Us

A Collect in Response to the Gospel Reading

(Spoken by a worship leader or in unison)

> Holy and Loving God,
> whose Spirit rested on Joseph,
> calling him to parenthood,
> and on Mary, preparing her for motherhood and birth,
> by your Spirit, call and prepare us
> for our relationships, our work, and our ministry,

that we also may say, "Your will be done in us,"
to the glory of Jesus Christ,
in whose name we pray. Amen.

Always You Are with Us

A Litany of Praise on the Meaning of "Emmanuel" (Isaiah 7:14 and
Matthew 1:23)

(Spoken responsively by two voices or by worship leader[s] and congregation. The bidding and response are the same phrase, spoken and then echoed, and printed in bold.)

Holy God, Emmanuel
always you are with us.
We are aware of you
only because you have created us
to know you and enjoy you for ever.

Covenant God, Emmanuel,
always you are with us.
You entered human history,
chose a particular people,
and walked with them in sorrow and joy.

Companion God, Emmanuel,
always you are with us.
You are the God of Abraham and Sarah,
Miriam and Moses,
Deborah and David,
Elizabeth and Zechariah,
Joseph and Mary.

Humble God, Emmanuel,
always you are with us,
now as one of us,
Jesus of Nazareth,
born of a woman,
with a face, a name, and a story.

Word in flesh, Emmanuel,
always you are with us.
We praise and adore you.
Amen.

CHAPTER 3

Advent Liturgies and Worship Elements

(YEAR B)

Liturgies for Placing an Advent Candle Ring and Lighting the Advent and Christ Candles

The Advent and Christ candles liturgies draw on the RCL Year B Advent and Christmas readings from Isaiah 64:1–9; Isaiah 40:1–11 and Psalm 85:8–13; Isaiah 61:1–4, 8–11; 2 Samuel 7:1–11, 16; Luke 1:26–38; Luke 1:46b–55; and Isaiah 9:2–7. For directions, see page 33.

First Sunday in Advent: Placing an Advent Candle Ring and Lighting the First Advent Candle

We shall light the Advent candles/place this candle ring,
praying that our preparation for Christmas may help us
to look outward in love,
and look forward in hope.
**Living Christ, light of the world,
give us the warmth of your love.**

(If a candle ring is used, set it in place.)

There are five candles.
We shall light a new candle each Sunday from now until
Christmas.

Candles are useful.
They give light and warmth when electricity fails.

Candles are simple, yet ingenious.
They show us the inventiveness of people in the past
and connect us with generations before us.

Candles are special.
In the dark, they give bright light and warm shadows.

Candlelight brings us together
as we talk and laugh and listen.
**Living Christ, light of the world,
give us the warmth of your love.**

In Isaiah, chapter 64, a prophet cries out to God:

O that you would tear open the heavens,
and come down, . . .
to make your name known. . . .
You have hidden your face from us. . . .
Yet . . . we are the clay, and you are our potter;
we are all the work of your hand.

(selections from Isa. 64:1–8)

We light our first candle
as a prayer for our suffering world,
that God, who is often hidden,
may be revealed to us and to all.

(Light the first candle.)

Living God, come to our world.
When you hide your face, help us,
to trust your promises and wait in hope.

Second Sunday in Advent: Lighting the Second Advent Candle
(Begin with the first candle relit.)

A prophet speaks, and a psalmist sings,
telling us how God will come:

Comfort my people, bring comfort to them,
    says your God. . . .
Clear a road through the wilderness. . . .
Prepare a highway across the desert for our God. . . .
Then will the glory of God be revealed
and all humankind shall see it. . . .

Love and faithfulness will come together.
Justice and peace will embrace.

(Isa. 40:1–11 and Ps. 85:10 REB*)

We light our second candle
as a prayer of hope and longing,
that God's glory may be revealed on earth,
through justice, peace, and faithful love.

(Light the second candle.)

Living God, come to our world.
Help us to recognize your presence
wherever people make peace,
show kindness, keep their promises,
and do what is right. Amen.

Third Sunday in Advent: Lighting the Third Advent Candle
(*Begin with the previous candles relit.*)

A prophet tells us how God comes—
through someone who receives God's spirit,
and through a community that hears the good news:

The Spirit of the Living God is upon me
because God has anointed me . . .
to announce good news to the humble,
to bind up the broken-hearted,
to proclaim liberty to captives,
and release to those in prison, . . .
to comfort all who mourn,
to give them garlands instead of ashes,
oil of gladness instead of mourners' tears.   (*Isa. 61:1–3 REB*)

We light our third candle,
as a sign of hope
that the Spirit of God may anoint us
to show God's liberating love.

(*Light the third candle.*)

Living God, proclaim liberty to captives.
Set us free, that we may free others.
Bind our wounds, that we may heal others.
Fill us with your Spirit,
and anoint us with your love.

Fourth Sunday in Advent: Lighting the Fourth Advent Candle
(*Begin with the previous candles relit.*)

God does not come from nowhere
but through a people named Israel,
a prophet named Nathan,
a king named David,
and a descendant of David named Jesus:

When King David had defeated his enemies
he wanted to build a temple, as a house for God's presence,
and consulted Nathan, who said,
"Do whatever you have in mind."
But God gave Nathan a different message
about a different kind of house:

Down to this day I have never dwelt in a house
since I brought Israel up out of Egypt.
I lived in a tent and a tabernacle. . . .
Your family and your kingdom
will be established for ever in my sight.   (*2 Sam. 7:6, 16 REB*)

Through an angel God speaks to Mary:
You will conceive and give birth to a son,
and you are to give him the name Jesus,
God will give him the throne of his ancestor David; . . .
his reign shall never end.   (*Luke 1:31, 33b REB*)

Through Mary, God speaks to us:
My spirit has rejoiced in God my Savior,
whose name is holy,
who has routed the proud and all their schemes,
brought down monarchs from their thrones, . . .
raised on high the lowly,
filled the hungry with good things,
and sent the rich away empty.
                    (*extracts from Luke 1:47–53 REB*)

We light our fourth candle,
as a sign of God's love,
shining in the world
through people past and present.

(*Light the fourth candle.*)

Living God, thank you for coming to our world.
Thank you for meeting us in real people,
whose stories we can tell,
and above all in Jesus.

Christmas Eve or Christmas Day: Lighting the Christ Candle

(*Begin with the previous candles relit.*)

In a time of violence and despair,
an ancient prophet gives good news:

The people that walked in darkness
have seen a great a light. . . .
The boots of earth-shaking armies on the march,
the soldiers' cloaks rolled in blood,
are destined to be burnt, food for the fire.
For a child has been born to us. . . .

Wide will be the dominion
and boundless the peace, . . .
with justice and righteousness
from now on, for evermore.   (*Isa. 9:2a, 5, 6a, 7a, 7c REB*)

We light the Christ candle,
thankful that God has come to us,
not as a conquering hero
but as a child, whose faithful, peaceful life
will follow God's way of love.

(*Light the Christ candle.*)

Living God, come to our world,
May the love of Christ shine brightly,
at the center of our lives,
spreading warmth and light,
in us, in this congregation, and everywhere.

Worship Elements for Particular Sundays

First Sunday in Advent

RCL READINGS: ISAIAH 64:1–9; PSALM 80:1–7, 17–19; 1 CORINTHIANS 1:3–9; MARK 13:24–37

Our Hope Is in the Name of Jesus

A Call to Worship or Affirmation of Faith for Years B and C, Based
on Mark 13:31 with 13:6–9 and Luke 21:33 with 21:25

*(Spoken by a worship leader or leaders, or by worship leader[s] and congregation. The
responding or congregation voice is printed in bold.)*

People of God, let us worship God:
In times of crisis and uncertainty,
some hide in fear,
dive into activity,
distract themselves with pleasure,
or sink into despair.
Some look for signs of the end
and count who they think will be saved.
But our hope is in the name of Jesus,
Jewish child of Jewish parents:
healing and teaching,
welcoming outcasts,
crucified by imperial power,
risen from the dead,
and endlessly alive.
Therefore, let us declare our faith:
Christ has died.
Christ is risen.
Christ will come again.
Thanks be to God!

The Art of Waiting

A Call to Worship or Discipleship

(Spoken by a worship leader)

Christmas comes, but not yet.
Before we celebrate, let us wait,
taking time to remember who is coming,

time to prepare our lives,
time to look outwards in love:
"Christmas waits to come.
Gently count the days:
time to wait and walk with God,
time to fill with praise." [1]

We Lay Our Lives before You

A Prayer of Commitment and Trust Drawn from Isaiah 64:4–5

(Spoken by a worship leader or leaders, or by worship leader[s] and congregation. The responding or congregation voice is printed in bold.)

Mysterious and Faithful God,
we lay our lives before you.
Come what may,
we will live our lives before you,
whether you speak or are silent,
are present or absent,
hidden or revealed.
From ages past, no one has heard,
no ear has perceived,
no eye has seen any God besides you.
So we will follow you, and trust
that you show your love to all who do right
and who remember your ways,
through Christ, your Word revealed.
Amen.

The Grace of God Has Been Given You

A Blessing and Promise from 1 Corinthians 1:4–8

(Spoken by a worship leader or leaders)

Friends, trust and believe the promises of God
through the apostle Paul:
The grace of God . . . has been given you in Christ Jesus,
for in every way you have been enriched in him,
in speech and knowledge of every kind, . . .
so that you are not lacking in any spiritual gift
as you wait for the revealing of our Lord Jesus Christ.

---

1. The quotation is from a worship song, "Christmas Waits to Come," by Susan Heafield and Brian Wren, awaiting publication.

God will also strengthen you to the end,
so that you may be blameless
on the day of our Lord Jesus Christ.
Thanks be to God! Amen!   (*1 Cor. 1:4–8*)

One Day at a Time

A Charge and Blessing Based on 1 Corinthians 1: 3–9

(*Spoken by a worship leader or leaders, or by worship leader[s] and congregation. The responding or congregation voice is printed in bold. The congregation may respond by echoing the response, "one day at a time."*)

In Jesus Christ, God's grace has been given to us;
therefore, let us live for God,
one day at a time.

In every way we have been enriched in Christ,
in spiritual gifts,
through the witness of those who showed us Christ,
and in speech and knowledge of every kind,
therefore, let us give thanks to God,
one day at a time.

God is faithful and will strengthen us to the end,
as we look for signs of Christ's presence,
one day at a time.

Till all is ended, all begun,
we live in hope and worship God,
one day at a time.

In the name of the Three who are One,
the Author, the Word, and the Breath,
go in peace.

Second Sunday in Advent

RCL READINGS: ISAIAH 40:1–11; PSALM 85:1–2, 8–13; 2 PETER 3:8–15A; MARK 1:1–8

Salvation Is at Hand

A Responsive Call to Worship Drawn from Psalm 85

(*Spoken by a worship leader or leaders, or by worship leader[s] and congregation. The responding or congregation voice is printed in bold.*)

People of God, dare to hope. Dare to believe.
Hear what God, the Living God, will speak,
for she will speak peace to her people.
   (OR: for God will speak peace to the people.)
Salvation is at hand for those who say, "Hallowed be your
    Name.
May your glory dwell in all lands."
Steadfast love and faithfulness will meet.
Justice and peace will kiss each other.
Fidelity will sprout from the earth,
and righteousness will lean down from heaven.

Come and Listen

An Advent Call to Worship

(Spoken by a worship leader or leaders)

Let us worship God.

Come and listen, come and sing, come and tell
how the Name beyond all names,
carpenter of all creation,
prepared to visit earth
by sending prophets and forerunners
and choosing a people, a place, a time, and a date
to risk being born.

Come and listen, come and sing, come and tell
how Joshua of Nazareth, Jesus,
named "Liberator," "Savior," and" God with us,"
was cradled by low-status parents
in a small town
far from the centers of power
in a superpower empire.

Come and listen, come and sing, come and tell
of birth and growth, teaching and healing,
betrayal and death, the day of resurrection,
and the coming of the Spirit!

Come and listen, come and sing, come and tell.
Come and worship God!

God Waits with Eternal Patience

A Call to Worship Drawn from 2 Peter 3:8–15a

(Use this in whole or in part, with one leader's voice or more.)

Come together in worship,
believing that God has a purpose
for every human being
and for all human histories.

Come together in worship
as God waits with eternal patience,
not wanting any to perish
but all to come to repentance.

Come, knowing that life is good—and life will end,
that our story on earth is unfinished, but will cease.

Since all things are to be dissolved,
what sort of persons should we be?

As sisters and brothers in Christ,
let us live at peace with each other,
in holiness and godliness
as we wait for new heavens and a new earth,
where righteousness is at home.

Contours of Repentance

A Collect Echoing the Old Testament and Gospel Readings

(Spoken by a worship leader or in unison)

Life-changing Spirit,
as we prepare the way for Christ,
outline the contours of our repentance—
in our life together as church,
in our relationships,
in our homes and beyond—
that our lives may be turned around,
more than we bargained for
but not less than we dared to hope,
through Jesus Christ. Amen.

For All Who Prepared the Way

A Litany of Thanksgiving

(Responsive or for two voices or for leader[s] and congregation. The responding or congregation voice is printed in bold. The bidding is printed in italics. Speak or sing the bidding and response.)

We praise you, Holy God,
for all who prepared the way
for Jesus, his life, and his ministry:

For Mary and Joseph,
who nursed, protected, and guided him,
accepting the vocation of parenthood,
and modeling your justice, kindness, and love,
and for the extended family and village community
that embraced and cherished him,
 we lift up our hearts
 in thanksgiving and praise.

For the prophets who inspired him
with visions of a Spirit-filled servant,
gathering outcasts,
bringing justice to the poor,
making and speaking peace,
and suffering to set us free,
 we lift up our hearts
 in thanksgiving and praise.

For Elizabeth and Zechariah,
and for their son, John,
who heard your word in the wilderness,
proclaimed it fearlessly to his people,
gathered disciples
and pointed them away from himself
to the One whose way he prepared,
 we lift up our hearts
 in thanksgiving and praise.

Third Sunday in Advent

RCL READINGS: ISAIAH 61:1–4, 8–11; PSALM 126; LUKE 1:47–55 (THE MAGNIFICAT—OPTIONAL); 1 THESSALONIANS 5:16–24; JOHN 1:6–8, 19–28

Our Mouths Were Filled with Laughter

A Responsive Call to Worship from Psalm 126

(*Spoken by a worship leader or leaders, or by worship leader[s] and congregation. The responding or congregation voice is printed in bold.*)

Let us worship God and take on our lips
words from a homecoming song:
When the Holy Name brought us home from captivity,
we thought we were dreaming.
Our mouths were filled with laughter then,
our tongues with songs of joy.

O God, Living God,
free our captive hearts.
Make them like streams in a desert.
May those who sow in tears
reap with shouts of joy.
May those who go out weeping,
bearing seed for sowing,
come home with shouts of joy,
carrying their sheaves.
Thanks be to God!

Come Together, People of God

A Call to Worship or Call to Discipleship (See the Third Sunday in Advent Year A on p. 44.)

Prayers Based on Isaiah 61:1–4, 8–11

(*Spoken by a worship leader or in unison*)

As You Anointed Jesus

A Collect

Holy God,
as you anointed Jesus with your Spirit
to comfort mourners,
bind up the brokenhearted,

proclaim release to prisoners
and bring good news to the oppressed,
so anoint us, as Christ's living body,
to go and do likewise.
Amen.

Holy Trinity, Wrapped in Light

A Petition

Holy Trinity, wrapped in light,
lover of justice,
opponent of robbery and wrong,
your scrutiny is inescapable,
your purity is unbearable,
and your love is immeasurable.
By the power of your Spirit,
cover us with robes of righteousness,
clothe us with garments of salvation,
and crown us with a garland of praise,
in the name of Christ. Amen.

We Rejoice and Exult

Praise and Adoration

Living and Loving God,
we praise and adore you
for calling us out of hiding,
accepting us in Christ,
forgiving our sin,
and setting us free.
With mind and body, heart and voice,
we rejoice and exult
that you are who you are,
for ever and ever. Amen.

By Your Sovereign Choice

A Collect

Everlasting Covenant God,
by your sovereign choice
we are yours.

Fill us with your Spirit
that the world may say,
"This is an undeserving people
whom God has blessed,"
through Christ, in whom we come and go,
and live and breathe. Amen.

Collects Drawn from John 1:6–8, 19–28

(*Spoken by a worship leader or in unison*)

Radiant Christ

Radiant Christ,
light of the world,
make us, your church,
a direction sign that points to you,
that because of us, and in spite of us,
people may see you and believe. Amen.

The Wisdom of John the Baptizer

Spirit of God,
give us the wisdom of John the Baptizer,
that in knowing who we are not,
we may find out who we are,
and be glad. Amen.

As Christ's New People

A Charge and Blessing Drawn from 1 Thessalonians 5:14–24

(*Spoken by a worship leader or leaders. Use one or more of the paragraphs marked P in the charge and end with the blessing.*)

Charge: As Christ's new people, freed and forgiven,

P   be at peace among yourselves.
Encourage those who lack confidence,
and be patient with everyone.
Let no-one repay evil for evil,
but seek to do good—to each other, and to all.

P   Rejoice always,
pray without ceasing,
and give thanks, whatever happens—

P   Hold fast to what is good,
respect the words of prophets;
test the wisdom of leaders;
abstain from evil;
and never quench the Spirit.

Blessing: May God, the God of peace,
make you holy, through and through,
and keep you sound in spirit, soul, and body,
free of any fault when the living Christ comes.

By the power of the Holy Spirit,
know that God is faithful
and will do this.
Go in God's peace. Amen.

Fourth Sunday in Advent

RCL READINGS: 2 SAMUEL 7:1–11, 16; LUKE 1:47–55 (THE MAGNIFICAT); PSALM 89:1–4, 19–26
(OPTIONAL ALTERNATIVE TO THE MAGNIFICAT); ROMANS 16:25–27; LUKE 1:26–38

We Will Sing of Your Love

**An Opening Act of Praise from Psalm 89:1–18, Including Verses
Omitted from the RCL Reading**

*(Spoken by a worship leader or leaders, or by worship leader[s] and congregation. The
responding or congregation voice is printed in bold.)*

O God, whose Name is wonderful,
we will sing of your love for ever,
and declare your faithfulness to all generations.
The universe is yours, and so is the earth.
You established them and all that they contain.
Your judgment seat is built on righteousness and justice.
Love and fidelity stand in your presence.
Happy are those who know how to praise you,
who walk in the light of your presence.
Hallelujah! Amen!

God on the Move

A Litany of Adoration Drawn from 2 Samuel 7:1–11, 16

(The bidding [in italics] and response [in bold] are for a worship leader and congregation [responsively] or two worship leaders. Speak or sing the bidding and response.)

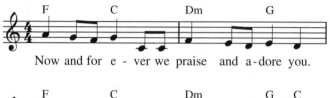

Now and for e - ver we praise and a-dore you.

Now and for e - ver we praise and a-dore you.

God on the move,
traveling with us,
pitching your tent
wherever we are,
yet out of our reach,
beyond definition,
eluding our grasp:
Now and for ever
we praise and adore you.

God in our midst,
God in the flesh,
pitching your tent
in a human life,
touched and seen,
with a face and a name,
exposed and at risk:
Now and for ever
we praise and adore you.

God of tomorrow,
end and beginning,
holding in memory
all that we are,

giving our living
motive and meaning,
judging, forgiving,
bringing us home:
Now and for ever
we praise and adore you.
Amen.

How Can a Baby Change the World?

A Meditative Prayer in Response to the Magnificat, Luke 1:47–55

(Spoken by a worship leader or leaders)

God, how can a baby change the world
even before it is born?
The proud seem quite secure,
the seats of power look unshaken.
The hungry are unfed,
and the rich take plenty away.
So how can a baby change the world?

And yet, when it stirs in the womb,
it changes somebody's world,
and when a child is born,
our lives are changed for ever.

Who knows, at birth, what a child will become?
Did Mary sing her song when her son left home,
when he sat on a hillside, hung on a cross,
and shattered the tomb?

Then how can a baby *not* change the world?
Who knows what a child will become?

For when, in a home or a nation,
new life surges, strong as the incoming tide,
it changes the shape of the shoreline
so that even the castles of power
are like sand.
Amen.

Three Collects from Luke 1:26–38

(Spoken by a worship leader or in unison)

The Space to Say "Yes"

Living God, Sovereign Love,
giving to Mary
anxious perplexity,
faith to believe,
and the space to say "Yes,"
keep us alert for visiting angels,
that we may hear your call,
be honest yet faithful,
and know that for you, nothing is impossible,
in Jesus Christ. Amen.

Courageous God

Courageous God,
putting your purpose for the world
in a teenage woman's body and hands,
give us, in youth and age,
young Mary's readiness for your call,
that we also may say:
"Here I am.
Let it be to me according to your word."
In the name of Christ we pray. Amen.

Recognizing Angels

God, it would be nice
to recognize angels
and say, "OK. Here am I."
But since you don't often come
with shining wings, in a flash of light,
give us your watchful Spirit
that we may resolve our perplexity,
detect your presence,
and answer your call,
through Jesus Christ. Amen.

To the Only Wise God

A Charge and Blessing from Romans 16:25–27

(Spoken by a worship leader or leaders, or by worship leader[s] and congregation. The responding or congregation voice is printed in bold.)

Sisters, brothers, friends,
the mystery kept secret for ages
is disclosed in the good news of Jesus.
**Amen. To the only wise God, through Jesus Christ,
may all give glory for ever!**

Through Jesus the Jew
and the writings of the prophets,
God's purpose is revealed—
to bring all earth's people
to freedom and hope
in the loving obedience of faith.
**Amen. To the only wise God, through Jesus Christ,
may all give glory for ever!**

Sisters, brothers, friends,
God is able to strengthen you.
Receive and spread the good news of Jesus,
and go in peace!
**Amen. To the only wise God, through Jesus Christ,
may all give glory for ever!**

CHAPTER 4

Advent Liturgies and Worship Elements

(YEAR C)

Liturgies for Placing an Advent Candle Ring and Lighting the Advent and Christ Candles

The Advent and Christ candles liturgies draw on the RCL Year C Advent and Christmas readings from Luke 21:25–36; Luke 3:1–6; Luke 1:39–45; Luke 2:15; and from Luke 3:15–16. For directions, see page 33.

First Sunday in Advent: Placing an Advent Candle Ring and Lighting the First Advent Candle

What are these candles for?

This is an Advent candle ring. It shows the circle of God's
   unbroken love.
   (OR: These Advent candles remind us of God's love in Jesus
   Christ.)

There are five candles.
We shall light a new candle each Sunday from now until
   Christmas.

What is the point of doing this?

Because the old proverb is true:
"What I hear, I forget.
What I see, I remember.
What I do, I understand."
As we light our Advent candles,
may they bring us together
in the warm light of God's love.

(If a candle ring is used, set it in place.)

The Gospel of Luke speaks about the future:
   "There will be signs in the sun, the moon, and the stars,
   and on the earth, distress among nations.
   People will faint from fear and foreboding." (*Luke 21:25–36*)

Because our world is full of fear and distress,
we light our first candle,
trusting that Christ is alive on earth
and that the Spirit of Christ lives among us.

(Light the first candle.)

> Living Christ, give us faith to trust you.
> **We trust you, we love you, we praise you. Amen.**

Second Sunday in Advent: Lighting the Second Advent Candle

(Begin with the first candle relit.)

> The Gospel of Luke speaks about God's messenger:
> In the fifteenth year
> of the reign of the Emperor Tiberius, . . .
> the word of God came to John son of Zechariah. . . .
> He went into all the region around the Jordan,
> proclaiming a baptism of repentance
> for the forgiveness of sins.   *(Luke 3:1–3)*

> God comes to us through particular people,
> in particular places and times
> in the past, and here and now.
> Our second candle reminds us
> to look for the light of God
> in God's messengers today.

(Light the second candle.)

> Living Christ, give us faith to trust you
> and hope to follow you.
> **We trust you, we love you, we praise you. Amen.**

Third Sunday in Advent: Lighting the Third Advent Candle

(Begin with the previous candles relit.)

> In the Gospel of Luke, John the Baptizer points to Jesus:
> As the people were filled with expectation, . . .
> questioning whether John might be the Messiah,
> John answered them by saying,
> "I baptize you with water,
> but one who is more powerful than I is coming. . . .
> He will baptize you
> with the Holy Spirit and fire."   *(Luke 3:15–16)*

> If we follow Jesus Christ,
> we will get everything we hope for,
> and more than we bargained for.
> We light our third candle to praise God,

whose Spirit comes to us
with disturbing and wonderful blessings.

(Light the third candle.)

Living Christ, give us faith to trust you,
hope to follow you,
and love to live for you.
We trust you, we love you, we praise you. Amen.

Fourth Sunday in Advent: Lighting the Fourth Advent Candle

(Begin with the previous candles relit.)

The Gospel of Luke tells how Mary meets her cousin
Elizabeth:
When Elizabeth heard Mary's greeting,
the child leaped in her womb.
And Elizabeth was filled with the Holy Spirit
and exclaimed with a loud cry,
"Blessed are you among women,
and blessed is the fruit of your womb."   (*Luke 1:41–42*)

God speaks in many ways:
through dreams, visions, new ideas,
and the kicking of a child not yet born.
We light our fourth candle,
asking that we may hear God's call
in our body, mind, and spirit.

(Light the fourth candle.)

Living Christ, give us faith to trust you,
hope to follow you,
love to live for you,
and wisdom to know you.
We trust you, we love you, we praise you. Amen.

Christmas Eve or Christmas Day: Lighting the Christ Candle

(Begin with the previous candles relit.)

The Gospel of Luke tells what happened
on the night when Jesus was born:

When the angels had left them, . . .
the shepherds said to one another,
"Let us go now to Bethlehem,
and see what has taken place,
which God has made known to us."   (*Luke 2:15*)

In those days, shepherds didn't count for much.
But God chose shepherds
to welcome and honor Jesus.
We light the Christ candle
to praise Jesus Christ, who comes to all of us,
beginning with the least and the last.

(*Light the Christ candle.*)

Living Christ, give us faith to trust you,
hope to follow you,
love to live for you,
wisdom to know you,
and joy to adore you.
We trust you, we love you, we praise you. Amen.

Worship Elements for Particular Sundays

First Sunday in Advent

RCL READINGS: JEREMIAH 33:14–16; PSALM 25:1–10; 1 THESSALONIANS 3:9–13; LUKE 21:25–36

Awake! Rejoice!

A Call to Worship

(Spoken responsively by two voices or by worship leader[s] and congregation. The responding or congregation voice is printed in bold.)

Awake! Rejoice!
Prepare to meet your God!
Christ is coming
Open the door.
Sweep the path.
Prepare the way!

Christ came at Christmas
to live as one of us.
Christ comes today
to love us and to lead us.
Christ will come tomorrow,
wherever we may be.

Christ will come when time and space are ended,
and everything returns to God.
Even so, come, Lord Jesus! Amen.

Upright and Good

A Responsive Call to Worship Drawn from Psalm 25

(Spoken responsively by two voices or by worship leader[s] and congregation. The responding or congregation voice is printed in bold.)

Let us worship God:
The Living God is upright and good,
leading the humble in the right direction
and instructing sinners in the right way.
God's pathways are made with faithfulness
and paved with steadfast love.

Living God, show us your ways
and teach us your paths.
**Remember us because of your love,
your ancient, unwavering love.
Amen.**

Living Christ, Jesus of Nazareth

A Collect for Advent

(Spoken by a worship leader or in unison)

Living Christ, Jesus of Nazareth,
Teacher and Friend, Savior and Lord,
we love you and long for your presence.
As we follow the story of your coming,
touch us by your Spirit,
that through people we know
and through people we have yet to meet,
we may hear your voice
and heed your call.
In your name we pray. Amen.

A Prayer for the Candor to Complain

This prayer is prompted by part of Psalm 26 but can be used also in
conjunction with laments such as Psalms 10, 13, 74, and 88.

*(Spoken responsively by two voices or by worship leader[s] and congregation. The responding
or congregation voice is printed in bold.)*

Holy God, hear our prayer
for all who know you only
as hidden, absent, or unavailable,
and for all whose experience testifies
that you have abandoned them
to suffering, abuse, and shame.
**Give them courage to cry out, like Israel of old,
to protest and complain
and demand that you keep your promises.**

Open our ears to hear their cry,
and give us the determination
to meet you, year by year,
choosing passion over politeness,

honesty over pretense,
questioning over silence,
covenant over divorce,
commitment over withdrawal,
and the courage to give you praise.
Amen.

Today's Captivities

A Litany

(Spoken responsively by two voices or by worship leader[s] and congregation. The bidding and response are the phrase, printed in bold, which is spoken and then echoed. Speak or sing the bidding and response.)

Sav-ior Christ, set us free! Sav-ior Christ, set us free!

Christ our Savior,
save us from today's captivities:

From the need to have more;
and from having our identity and self-worth
defined by what we possess—
Savior Christ, set us free.

From the need to be satisfied without waiting;
and from anxiety when material longings are deferred—
Savior Christ, set us free.

From paralysis and confusion,
in the face of so many needs, so much information—
Savior Christ, set us free.

From hyperactivism that denies our limitations,
and from apathy that denies our God-given powers—
Savior Christ, set us free.

From trying to replace you as Savior,
by taking the world on our shoulders—
Savior Christ, set us free.

From ignorance or denial of what drives us;
and from captivity to personal drives and needs—
Savior Christ, set us free.

From embarrassment in speaking about your love;
from not knowing what to say;
and from the shame of being misunderstood, scorned, or
　　　ignored—
Savior Christ, set us free.

From captivity to anger, bitterness, and disappointment;
and from captivities we cannot speak about, or name—
Savior Christ, set us free. Amen

Second Sunday in Advent

RCL READINGS: MALACHI 3:1–4; LUKE 1:68–79; PHILIPPIANS 1:3–11; LUKE 3:1–6

Raise Your Voices, Lift Up Your Hearts

A Call to Worship from Luke 1:68–79

(*Spoken responsively by two voices or by worship leader[s] and congregation. The responding or congregation voice is printed in bold.*)

Raise your voices, lift up your hearts.
Praise the One, the only One, life-giving God of Israel:
You have turned to your people and set them free.
You have raised a strong deliverer
from the house of your servant David.

Raise your voices, lift up your hearts.
Thank God for the messengers of hope,
who bring knowledge of salvation
by the forgiveness of sins.

Raise your voices, lift up your hearts.
An ancient promise is fulfilled:
On people who live in a dark night,
under the shadow of death,
the dawn from heaven breaks
to free us all from fear
and guide our feet into the way of peace.
Praise God! Praise God! Amen!

God Most Particular

A Collect Responding to Luke 3:1–6

(Spoken by a worship leader or in unison)

God most particular,
descending from generalities
to show yourself in person,
and speak to John the Baptizer
in a particular time and place,
make our love for you
as particular and specific
as your love for us,
beginning here, beginning now,
through the leveler of mountains
and the straightener of crooked ways,
Jesus Christ.
Amen.

Who Cares, God?

A Meditative Prayer Responding to Luke 3:1–6

(Spoken by a worship leader; this is not suitable for unison speech.)

Who cares, God,
which calendar Luke was using,
whether his governors, princes, and priests
are accurate in every detail,
and whether John went to the desert
in October, March, or June?
All we need to know
is that around that time
and about that place,
a voice cried out in the desert,
and we must decide
whether to listen
and what to do.
Amen.

God, Our Owner and Creator

An Offering Prayer Drawing on Philippians 1:5–6

(Spoken by a worship leader or in unison)

God, our Owner and Creator,
we return to you thanks
for life and breath
and for your gifts of strength and skill,
of money, wisdom, hope, and love.
Use our tangible gratitude
to extend our sharing of the gospel,
until you bring to completion
the good work you have begun in us,
through Jesus Christ. Amen.

All the Saints Surround Us

A Charge and Blessing Drawing on Philippians 1:7–11

(Spoken by a worship leader or leaders)

We are not alone.
All the saints surround us
with the compassion of Christ Jesus.
Therefore, go out in hope,
and may love overflow more and more
with knowledge and insight
to help us determine what is best,
that the Spirit may reap in us
the harvest of righteousness,
for the glory and praise of God
through Jesus Christ.
Amen.

Third Sunday in Advent

RCL READINGS: ZEPHANIAH 3:14–20; ISAIAH 12:2–6; PHILIPPIANS 4:4–7; LUKE 3:7–18

Shout Aloud and Sing for Joy![1]

A Call to Worship or Joyful Acclamation Quilted from Isaiah 12, John 1, 1 Corinthians 15, Colossians 2, and 1 Peter 2.

(Spoken responsively by two voices, a choir, or a speaking team [see p. xiv] or by worship leader[s] and congregation. Use all or make a selection. The responding or congregation parts are in bold.)

1. Also suitable for Years A, B, and C at the Easter Vigil.

Give thanks to the One Who Lives. . . .
Declare God's deeds among the nations!
The Word became flesh and lived among us, . . .
full of grace and truth.
Shout aloud and sing for joy,
for great in our midst is the Holy One of Israel.

Christ has been raised from the dead,
the first fruits of those who have died.
The Holy Name is our strength and our might
and has become our salvation.

On the cross Christ disarmed the rulers and authorities
and made a public example of them.
Sing praises to the Living God, for God has triumphed.
Let this be known in all the world.

Christ himself bore our sins in his own body on the cross
so that, free from sins, we might live for righteousness.
Surely God is our salvation.
We will trust and will not be afraid.

With joy draw water from the wells of deliverance
and say on this day:
God is our deliverer.
We will be confident and unafraid!

(*The exact references are Isa. 12:4b; John 1:14; Isa. 12:6; 1 Cor.
15:20; Isa. 12:2b*; Col. 2:15; Isa. 12:5 REB; 1 Pet. 2:24; Isa.
12:2a; Isa. 12:3–4a REB*; and Isa. 12:2a REB.*)

The Living God Is in Our Midst

A Call to Worship Drawn from Zephaniah 3:14–20

(*Spoken by a worship leader or leaders*)

Listen to words of promise and hope
and share the great good news:
God is not distant or uncaring,
but moves with loving power
to meet us as we meet.

The Living God is in our midst
to rejoice over us with gladness,

renew us in love,
and lift us up with words of hope:

I will remove disaster from you.
I will deal with oppressors,
rescue the lame,
and gather the outcast.
I will bring you home forever
and change your shame into honor and praise.

Thanks be to God!

Prayers in Response to Philippians 4:4–9

(The following prayers use the whole reading. RCL has only 4:4–7.)

Caregiving God

A Collect

(Spoken by a worship leader or in unison)

Caregiving God,
providing for our needs,
as you long to fill the hungry with food,
so also fill our imagination
with people and things that are just and true,
excellent, noble, and worthy of praise,
that by dwelling on the beauty of goodness,
we may grow into it day by day
as students of Christ
in whose name we pray. Amen.

When Worry Devours Our Strength

A Petition

(Spoken by a worship leader or in unison)

In the stress and strain of life,
when worry devours our strength,
burdens are hard to bear,
and floodwaters tug at our feet,
give us, Compassionate God,
solid ground to stand on,

helping hands for heavy loads,
and when we least expect it,
the peace that surpasses understanding,
through Jesus Christ.
Amen.

God of Surpassing Peace

A Collect

(Spoken by a worship leader or in unison)

God of surpassing peace,
give us and all your church,
peace of mind, forgiving peace,
and reconciling peace.
Inscribe their signatures
in muscle, brain, and bone,
so that we may know, share, and give
the peace beyond understanding
that the world cannot give.
In Christ's name we pray. Amen.

Always Rejoice in Christ

A Charge and Blessing Drawn from Philippians 4:4–9)

(Spoken by a worship leader or leaders)

Always rejoice in Christ.
Again I say, Rejoice!
Ask God for what you need,
simply, directly, trustingly,
and always with thanksgiving.
Imitate what you have learned and received
and heard and seen
in the Scriptures and the saints,
and be assured that the peace of God,
which cannot be grasped or measured,
will guard our hearts and minds in Christ Jesus.
Go out in peace—Christ's peace. Amen.

Fourth Sunday in Advent

RCL READINGS: MICAH 5:2–5A; LUKE 1:47–55; PSALM 80:1–7; HEBREWS 10:5–10; LUKE 1:39–45 (46–55)

Speak of the Promise That Calls Us

A Call to Worship Drawn from Micah 5:2–5a

(Spoken responsively by two voices or by worship leader[s] and congregation. The responding or congregation voice is printed in bold.)

Welcome. Worship God.
Speak of the promise that calls us.

From a village called Bethlehem
comes a leader, God-beloved,
to govern God's people—
to lead us as a shepherd guides the flock
to water and good pasture.

With origins deep in the past,
comes a child about to be born,
the source of true security—
whose greatness shall reach
to the ends of the earth,
bringing peace.

How Can We Stand in the Presence of God?

A Call to Worship or Invitation to Communion Prompted by Hebrews 10:1–10

(Spoken in the form of a dialogue and affirmation. The lectionary uses only vv. 5–10. Spoken by several voices or by worship leader[s] and congregation, whose voice is printed in bold.)

Friends, we are always in God's presence.
Yet how can we stand in the presence of God?

The Living God is pure
and holy beyond measure,
but we are stained with wrongdoing.
We have impure hearts.

No matter how good we are,
we cannot remove the stain.

Before Christ came, our ancestors in faith offered animal
    sacrifices
and received God's cleansing love.

But each time an animal was slaughtered,
its death was a vivid reminder
that there would be a next time, and a next, and a next,
because no-one could be permanently clean.

**The good news, then and now,
is that the death of Christ on the cross
is God's final act of cleansing
and needs no repetition.**

In Christ, God, who is holy,
reached out to gather the outcasts
and make a welcome table
where no-one is called unclean.

Therefore, believe in your heart
and say out loud to the world:

**In Christ, our sins are forgiven
and no-one is outcast or unclean,
for through the offering of Christ's body,
God has made us holy and clean, once for all.
Thanks be to God. Amen.**

Exuberant, Life-Giving God

A Collect Drawn from Luke 1:39–45

(Spoken by a worship leader or in unison)

Exuberant, Life-Giving God,
as Elizabeth, filled with the Spirit,
was moved to bless Mary's child,
so fill us with your Spirit
that our neighbors' hidden hopes
may be blessed and brought to birth,
to the glory of your name,
through the fruit of Mary's womb,
Jesus Christ.
Amen.

Let Go of the Burden of Uncleanness

A Charge and Trinitarian Blessing Prompted by Hebrews 10:1–10

(Spoken by a worship leader or leaders)

Through Christ our sins are forgiven
and no-one is outcast or unclean.
So go, at peace, and in peace.
Let go of the burden of uncleanness,
and do not inflict it on anyone.
Proclaim and live the great good news
that Christ hosts a welcome table
where all may gather in peace
to listen, speak, and sing,

And may the blessing of God,
the Welcoming Word, the All-Cleansing Spirit,
and the Radiance of Original Love
rest and remain with you all. Amen.

CHAPTER 5

What Child Is This?

A CHRISTMAS SERVICE OF SCRIPTURE AND SONG

(YEAR A)

This service can be used in any year.
For lectionary users, the appropriate year is specified.

General Introduction

The idea of a Christmastide service of Scripture readings and songs goes back to 1918 when Eric Milner-White, newly appointed Dean of King's College, Cambridge, England, devised a service of "Nine Lessons and Carols" for Christmas Eve. Experience as a wartime chaplain had convinced him that the Church of England needed more-imaginative worship.[1] As often happens, innovation hardened into fixed "tradition." The Scripture readings in the King's College service have continued unchanged since 1919. Only its music shows variation and innovation.

Magnificent as it may be, the King's College service has limitations. Taken from the (Authorized) King James Version, the archaism of its Scripture selections confines users to a ghetto of romantic religiosity that turns its back on the communicative power of twentieth-century English translations like the Revised English Bible, New Jerusalem Bible, New Revised Standard Version, Today's English Version, and others.

An equally serious limitation is that the King's service articulates one and only one strand of Christian theology, a story line of creation-fall-redemption that harks back to a pre-Copernican universe. Worship limited to this story line ignores other important biblical themes. The outlines in this and the following chapters illustrate the richness of scriptural traditions available for such a service. Because Christmas is a time for familiar ritual, there is some repetition from year to year. Hymn suggestions are mostly traditional, because congregations look for familiar songs at Christmastime. If these outlines encourage you to use or adapt them by shortening the readings, to choose other readings and more recent hymns and songs, or to prepare something different and better, they will have done their work.

The outlines can accommodate instrumental preludes, choral songs and solos, drama, dance, and visual arts. Each outline leaves space for lighting the Christ candle and completing the process begun in Advent by those who use the Advent candles liturgies in chapters 2–4. Each service optionally includes an Advent-to-Christmas theme song suitable but not limited to one of the lectionary years. Words and music are on pages 16–23 in chapter 1. The songs are as follows:

"Someone Comes"	Compatible with Advent Year A
"Great Holy One"	Compatible with Advent Year B
"Rejoice, Give Thanks"	Compatible with Advent Year C

---

1. The 1918 service was adapted from an Order of Worship drawn up by E. W. Benson, then Bishop of Truro, for use in the wooden shed that then served as the cathedral, at 10:00 p.m. on Christmas Eve 1880. His son A. C. Benson recalled, "My father arranged from ancient sources a little service for Christmas Eve—nine carols and nine tiny lessons, which were read by various officers of the Church, beginning with a chorister, and ending, through the different grades, with the Bishop." The suggestion had come from G. H. S. Walpole, later Bishop of Edinburgh.

Each act of worship also includes an optional time when candles are the only light. Candles are given to worshipers on arrival and used as indicated. For safety, the candlelit time is short.

Scripture readings are printed in full and cast into sense lines for ease of reading, as explained in the introduction to this book (p. xiv above).

What Child Is This?

(The theme song of this service is published in many hymnals to the tune GREENSLEEVES. Text and tune are in the public domain, may be reproduced without fee, and are printed below. The words are by William Chatterton Dix [ca. 1865] with minor amendments. For the tune, see p. 88.)

What child is this who, laid to rest
on Mary's lap is sleeping,
whom angels greet with anthems sweet,
while shepherds watch are keeping?
This, this is Christ the King,
whom shepherds guard and angels sing.
Haste, haste, to sing his praise,
the babe, the son of Mary.

Why lies he in such low estate
where ox and ass are feeding?
Good Christians, fear: For sinners here
the silent Word is pleading.
Nails, spear shall pierce him through,
the cross be borne for me, for you.
Hail, hail the Word made flesh,
the babe, the son of Mary.

So bring him incense, gold, and myrrh,
come poor and rich to own him.
The end of kings salvation brings,
let loving hearts enthrone him.
Raise, raise a song on high,
then hush to sing his lullaby.
Joy, joy for Christ is born,
the babe, the son of Mary.

Tune: GREENSLEEVES
English Melody, pre-1642
Poetic Meter: 8.7.8.7.6.8.6.7

Order of Service

Greeting and Call to Worship

(Spoken by a worship leader or leaders, or by worship leader[s] and congregation. The responding or congregation voice is printed in bold.)

> Do not be afraid.
> I bring you good news of great joy, for all people.
> To you is born this day, in the city of David,
> a Savior, who is the Messiah, the Lord.
>
> **There is nothing in death or life,**
> **in things present, or things to come,**
> **nothing in all creation,**
> **that can separate us from the love of God,**
> **in Christ Jesus our Lord.**
>
> Rejoice in the Lord always,
> and again I say, Rejoice!
> **Thanks be to God! Amen!**
>
> (Luke 2:11; Rom. 8:38–39*; Phil. 4:4)

Entrance Song: "Someone Comes"

(For words and music, see pp. 9 and 16.)

Hymn: "Joy to the World"

(AHB, BP, CH, CH4, ELW, H82, NCH, PH, RJS, UMH, VU)

or "Long Ago, Prophets Knew"

(AHB, AMNS, BP)

Prayer: "God of Peace," A Gathering Prayer

(Spoken by a worship leader or in unison)

> God of peace,
> you hold the nations in your hand,
> yet know and love us all.
> By your Spirit, you gather us;
> in Christ, you make us one.
> As we come together,
> show us who we are,
> what we can be,

and where we should go,
through Jesus Christ,
our Rescuer, Partner, and Friend. Amen.

Lighting the Christ Candle Year A
(Optional; see p. 52.)

Who Is This Child?

Introduction
(Spoken by a worship leader or leaders)

Tonight, we shall tell the story of God's love in Jesus Christ,
in Scripture, poetry, and song.
Our theme is taken from a Christmas song
as we begin by asking,
"What child is this, who laid to rest,
on Mary's lap is sleeping,
whom angels greet with anthems sweet
while shepherds watch are keeping?"
Who is this child? What message does he bring?
What kind of leadership? What way of living for today?

First Reading: Glory Revealed to All (Isaiah 40:1–5)
(Spoken by one or more people)

The prophet Isaiah promises that God's glorious love
will be revealed to all humankind:
　　Comfort, O comfort my people, says your God.
　　Speak tenderly to Jerusalem,
　　　　and cry to her
　　that she has served her term,
　　　　that her penalty is paid,
　　that she has received from the hand of God
　　　　double for all her sins.

　　A voice cries out:
　　"In the wilderness prepare the way of the Living God.
　　　　Make straight in the desert a highway for our God.
　　Every valley shall be lifted up,
　　　　and every mountain and hill be made low;
　　the uneven ground shall become level,
　　　　and the rough places a plain.

Then the glory of the Living God shall be revealed,
and all people shall see it together,
for the mouth of God has spoken."

Christ is coming. Be glad and believe.

Hymn: "Hail to the Lord's Anointed"
(AHB, AMNS, BP, CH, CH4, ELW, H82, NCH, RJS, UMH, VU)
or "Comfort, Comfort You My People"
(AHB, BP, CH, CH4, ELW, NCH, PH, VU)

Second Reading: A Servant with Gentle Strength
(Isaiah 42:1–4 REB)
(*Spoken by one or more people*)

The prophet Isaiah proclaims God's chosen One,
whose gentle strength will put things right.

Here is my servant, whom I uphold,
my chosen one, in whom I take delight!
I have put my spirit on him;
he will establish justice among the nations.
He will not shout or raise his voice,
or make himself heard in the street.
He will not break a crushed reed
or snuff out a smoldering wick;
unfailingly he will establish justice.
He will never falter or be crushed
until he sets justice on earth,
while coasts and islands await his teaching.

Christ is coming. Be glad and believe.

Hymn: "Angels We Have Heard on High"
(BP, CH, ELW, H82, NCH, PH, UMH, VU)
or "Angels From the Realms of Glory"
(AHB, AMNS, BP, CH, CH4, ELW, H82, NCH, PH, RJS, UMH, VU)

Third Reading: Equal, Beloved, and United
(Galatians 4:4–7 and 3:27–28)
(*Spoken by one or more people*)

The apostle Paul tells us
how Christ makes us God's children,
equal, beloved, and united:

> But when the fullness of time had come, God sent his Son,
> born of a woman, born under the law,
> in order to redeem those who were under the law,
> so that we might receive adoption as children.
> And because you are children,
> God has sent the Spirit of his Son into our hearts,
> crying, "Abba! Father!"
> So you are no longer a slave but a child,
> and if a child then also an heir, through God.

> As many of you as were baptized into Christ
> have clothed yourselves with Christ.
> There is no longer Jew or Greek,
> there is no longer slave or free,
> there is no longer male and female;
> for all of you are one in Christ Jesus.

Christ is coming. Be glad and believe.

Hymn: "What Child Is This?" (Stanza 2)

Why Lies He in Such Low Estate?

Introduction
(Spoken by a worship leader)

> Why lies he in such low estate, where ox and ass are sleeping?
> Good Christians, fear: For sinners here
> the silent Word is pleading.
> What does it mean that Jesus was born
> not in a palace or comfortable home
> but outside, in a cave for farm animals?

Fourth Reading: A Servant of Peace Is Born (Luke 2:1–7)
(Spoken by one or more people)

> Against the backdrop of an imperial, occupying power
> counting its subject population
> in order to levy taxes,
> a servant of peace is born:

In those days a decree went out from Emperor Augustus
that all the world should be registered.
This was the first registration
and was taken while Quirinius was governor of Syria.
All went to their own towns to be registered.
Joseph also went from the town of Nazareth in Galilee to
    Judea,
to the city of David called Bethlehem,
because he was descended from the house and family of
    David.
He went to be registered with Mary,
to whom he was engaged and who was expecting a child.
While they were there, the time came for her to deliver her
    child.
And she gave birth to her firstborn son,
wrapped him in bands of cloth,
and laid him in a manger,
because there was no place for them in the inn.

Christ has come. Rejoice and receive.

Introduction to the Next Hymn and Reading

(Spoken by a worship leader)

In the time of Jesus, shepherds were looked down on.
They worked irregular hours.
They didn't often get to synagogue.
They were regarded as uncouth and unclean.
What does it mean that Jesus was recognized, honored, and
    adored
not by the Town Council and the Chamber of Commerce,
but by people called unclean?
Let us sing their story:

Hymn: "While Shepherds Watched"

(AHB, AMNS, BP, CH, CH4 ["While Humble Shepherds Watched"], H82, PH, RJS, UMH, VU)

or "Mimgxing canlan ye wei yang"

["Midnight Stars Make Bright the Skies"—ELW];

"Hitsuji wa nemureri"

["Sheep Fast Asleep"—NCH];

or "Pastores a Belén"

["As Shepherds Filled with Joy—NCH.]

Fifth Reading: Adored by Outsiders (Luke 2:15–21)
(Spoken by one or more people)

When the angels had left them and gone into heaven,
the shepherds said to one another,
"Let us go now to Bethlehem and see this thing that has
taken place,
which God has made known to us."
So they went with haste and found Mary and Joseph,
and the child lying in the manger.
When they saw this,
they made known what had been told them about this
child;
and all who heard it were amazed at what the shepherds
told them.
But Mary treasured all these words and pondered them in
her heart.
The shepherds returned,
glorifying and praising God for all they had heard and
seen,
as it had been told them.
After eight days had passed,
it was time to circumcise the child;
and he was called Jesus [which means "Liberator,"
"Deliverer"],
the name given by the angel before he was conceived in the
womb.

Christ has come. Rejoice and receive.

Sung Solo, Hymn, or Spoken Poem: "Her Baby, Newly Breathing"
(See p. 139.)

Sixth Reading: Taking the Form of a Slave (Philippians 2:5–11)
(Spoken by one or more people)

How can the fullness of the divine,
far beyond our imagination,
be expressed in the confines of one human being,
one human life—
"unstinting, unprotected
prepared for nail and thorn,
constricted into maleness,
and of a woman born"?
(*Quoted from the hymn "Her Baby, Newly Breathing [see p. 139]*)

A poem by the apostle Paul tells the story:

> Let the same mind be in you that was in Christ Jesus,
> who, though he was in the form of God,
> did not regard equality with God
> as something to be exploited,
> but emptied himself,
> taking the form of a slave,
> being born in human likeness.
> And being found in human form,
> he humbled himself
> and became obedient to the point of death—
> even death on a cross.
> Therefore God also highly exalted him
> and gave him the name
> that is above every name,
> so that at the name of Jesus
> every knee should bend,
> in heaven and on earth and under the earth,
> and every tongue should confess
> that Jesus Christ is Lord,
> to the glory of God the Father. (*Phil. 2:5–11*)
> Christ has come. Rejoice and receive.

(For a new hymn on this passage, see "Christ, You Did Not Sit with God," p. 131.)

Hymn: "O Come, All Ye Faithful"

(AHB, AMNS, BP, CH, CH4, ELW, H82, NCH, PH, RJS, UMH, VU)

Let Loving Hearts Enthrone Him!

Introduction: "The Reign of Christ," An Affirmation of Faith

(Spoken by a worship leader or leaders or by worship leader[s] and congregation. The responding or congregation voice is printed in bold.)

> The reign of Christ comes not by conquest, domination, and
> manipulation,
> but by gracious love, gladly given, and willingly received.
> The reign of Christ comes near wherever people covenant
> together and say,
> **Christ, we are your body: live in our hearts.**
> **Christ, we are your people: govern our lives.**
> **Christ, we are your witnesses: send us out in your name!**

Hymn: "What Child Is This?" (Stanza 3)

Seventh Reading: Royal Robes for a Rescued People (Colossians 2:6 and 3:12–15)

(Spoken by one or more people)

Paul reminds us that the story of Jesus
is not just a tale to be told
but a new way of living.

As you have received Christ Jesus the Lord,
continue to live your lives in him,
rooted and built up in him
and established in the faith, just as you were taught,
abounding in thanksgiving.

As God's chosen ones, holy and beloved,
clothe yourselves with compassion, kindness,
humility, meekness, and patience.
Bear with one another and,
if anyone has a complaint against another,
forgive each other;
just as the Lord has forgiven you, so you also must forgive.

Above all, clothe yourselves with love,
which binds everything together in perfect harmony.
And let the peace of Christ rule in your hearts,
to which indeed you were called in the one body.
And be thankful.

Christ is the Way, the Truth, and the Life.
Rejoice, believe, and follow.

Hymn: "Hark, the Herald Angels Sing!"
(AHB, AMNS, BP, CH, CH4, ELW, H82, NCH, PH, RJS, UMH, VU)

Eighth Reading: A Jew for All Peoples (Luke 2:25–32)

(Spoken by one or more people)

Luke tells us how Jesus, the Jew,
came to his own people,
to reach out to all the world.

Now there was a man in Jerusalem whose name was
    Simeon;
this man was righteous and devout,
looking forward to the consolation of Israel,
and the Holy Spirit rested on him.
It had been revealed to him by the Holy Spirit
that he would not see death
before he had seen the Lord's Messiah.

Guided by the Spirit, Simeon came into the temple;
and when the parents brought in the child Jesus,
to do for him what was customary under the law,
Simeon took him in his arms and praised God, saying,
    "Master, now you are dismissing your servant in peace,
      according to your word;
  for my eyes have seen your salvation,
    which you have prepared in the presence of all
    peoples,
  a light for revelation to the Gentiles
    and for glory to your people Israel."

Christ is the Way, the Truth, and the Life.
Rejoice, believe, and follow.

Lighting of All Candles
(*Spoken by a worship leader*)

Christ, the light of the world, gives each one of us light,
so that we too may shine
with gratitude, hope, and love.
Receive the light that comes to you:
it comes from the Christ candle,
but it reaches you only through your neighbors.
Receive the light from a brother or sister in Christ.
Hold the light, enjoy the light, and be thankful.

(*Main lights are switched off. Candle lighters then take their light from the Christ candle and move down the aisle[s], lighting the candles at the end of each row; each person passes the light to his or her neighbor.*)

Hymn: "Silent Night"
(*It is easier to sing this familiar hymn while holding a candle if the words are projected on a screen or printed on a sheet of paper that can be held in one hand. Both versions below are public domain and can be reproduced without charge. For the tune, see your own hymnal.*)

A Traditional Version

Silent night, holy night,
all is calm, all is bright
round yon virgin mother and child.
Holy infant, so tender and mild,
sleep in heavenly peace. (times 2)

Silent night, holy night,
shepherds quake at the sight;
glories stream from heaven afar,
heavenly hosts sing Alleluia!
Christ the Savior is born. (times 2)

Silent night, holy night,
Son of God, love's pure light;
radiant beams from thy holy face
with the dawn of redeeming grace,
Jesus, Lord, at thy birth. (times 2)

An Updated Version

Silent night, holy night,
all is calm, all is bright.
Mary, cradle your newborn son,
smile and sing, love's labor done.
"Sleep in heavenly peace." (times 2)

Silent night, holy night,
angels stand, robed in light,
singing, "Shepherds, do not fear.
Alleluia! God is here.
Christ the Savior is born." (times 2)

Silent night, holy night,
all is good, all is right:
Word eternal, full of grace,
shining in a human face,
Jesus, live in our hearts. (times 2)

—*Brian Wren* (*in public domain*)

"Come to Me," A Call to Prayer

(Spoken by a worship leader or leaders)

> The living Christ invites us:
> "Come to me, all who are weary
> and carrying heavy burdens,
> and I will give you rest.
> Take my yoke upon you, and learn from me;
> for my yoke is easy, and my burden is light.
>
> *(Matt. 11:28, 30*)*

"Christ among Us," A Petition

> Christ among us, Light of the World,
> heal our brokenness, and bring us to wholeness,
> ease our pain, and bring us hope, strength, and life.
> Give us new heart, new hope, and a new song,
> that our prayers and deeds may be one.
> We ask it in your name. Amen.

Ninth Reading: Love's Living Word (John 1:1–13, 18)

(Spoken by one or more people)

> The first chapter of John's Gospel invites us to ponder the
>   wonder
> of Love's eternal mystery, touched, and seen in the flesh:

> In the beginning
> the Word already was.
> The Word was in God's presence,
> and what God was, the Word was.

> The Word was with God at the beginning,
> and through the Word all things came to be.
> In the Word was life,
> and that life was the light of humankind.
> The light shines in the darkness,
> and the darkness has never mastered it.

> There appeared a man named John, sent from God.
> He was not himself the light;
> he came to bear witness to the light.

> The true light which gives light to everyone
> was even then coming into the world.

So the Word became flesh and was at home among us;
and we saw the Word's glory, . . .
full of grace and truth.   (*John 1:1–6, 8–9, 14a, c REB**)

Christ is the Way, the Truth, and the Life.
Rejoice, believe, and follow.

Blow out your candles now,
but take the light of Christ with you
out into the world.

(*Main lights are switched on. Candles are extinguished.*)

Hymn: "Go, Tell It on the Mountain!"
(BP, CH, ELW, H82, NCH, PH, RJS, UMH, VU)
or "O For a Thousand Tongues to Sing"
(AHB, AMNS, CH4)

"Go in Peace!" A Blessing

Go in peace.
May the love that made the stars,
be your guiding light.
May the love revealed in Jesus
be your hope and inspiration;
and may the love of the ever-present Spirit,
give you courage, joy, and hope,
now and for ever. Amen.

CHAPTER 6

Show Us Who You Are

A CHRISTMAS SERVICE OF SCRIPTURE AND SONG

(YEAR B)

This service can be used in any year.
For lectionary users, the appropriate year is specified.

"It Came upon the Midnight Clear"

"It Came upon the Midnight Clear" is suggested on page 110 and appears in many hymnals. Because many of the standard versions have text and tune problems, I look at it more closely now. (For the original text, see the appendix.)

In December 1849, Edmund H. Sears, a Unitarian minister in Wayland, Massachusetts, wrote a poem titled "Christmas Carol," published on December 29 in Boston's *Christian Register*. Its five stanzas develop the theme of the angel song of peace on earth (Luke 1:8–14), with a recurring emphasis on whether or not people listen to the song.

The poem was written in the aftermath of the 1845–48 Mexican-American War. Throughout the preceding year, revolutionary movements had swept Europe. In the United States, slavery was becoming a hot issue, and there was growing agitation at the low wages, long hours, poor safety, and grinding poverty of industrial workers and child laborers. Whether or not these events prompted the hymn, it came from the pen of a minister whose church tradition had and has an active social conscience, and its peace theme was insistent and unmistakable.

During its 150-year journey, several issues have prompted revision. Because Christian hope is in God's purpose, not in a "golden age," and because the word "bards" is—except in Wales—archaic, Sears's original lines "by prophet-bards foretold . . . comes round the age of gold" have been amended to "by prophets seen of old, . . . shall come the time foretold." The archaism of "lowly" and its juxtaposition with "sad" led one hymnal to make a useful change from "sad and lowly plains" to "sad and lonely plains." Most hymnals change "Peace on the earth, goodwill to men" to ". . . goodwill to all" or something similar.

Some important problematic issues have received less attention, however. Sears's original fourth stanza opens with a picture of people carrying a load, apparently up a mountain ("climbing way"). This image vaguely suggests a hike on the Appalachian Trail. The assurance that "glad and golden hours come swiftly on the wing" is closer to Pollyanna optimism than Christian faith. In a four-stanza selection, which most hymnals now make, this stanza is the most suitable candidate for omission.

A more serious alteration is the widespread omission of Sears's third stanza in American hymnals (British and Canadian hymnals retain it). The original reads,

> But with the woes of sin and strife
>   the world has suffered long;
> beneath the angel-strain have rolled
>   two thousand years of wrong;
> and man, at war with man, hears not
>   the love song which they bring:
> O hush the noise, ye men of strife,
>   and hear the angels sing!

This stanza is the keystone of the hymn, and its omission negates Sears's insistent focus on interhuman peace contrasted with interhuman conflict. Culprit hymnals should reinstate this stanza, repairing its nowadays-sexist references to "men of strife" and "man at war with man."

Another major problem is the customary American tune CAROL, originally composed by Richard Willis for Philip Doddridge's hymn "See Israel's Gentle Shepherd Stand." CAROL is a waltz lullaby well matched with Doddridge's text but at variance with the impassioned testimony of "It Came upon the Midnight Clear." To omit Sears's third stanza and use this tune sentimentalizes the hymn and disrespects the author's intention. A more suitable tune is Arthur Sullivan's NOEL, long in public domain and the standard choice in British collections.

My textual revision updates the hymn's language and repairs some of its archaisms. It is printed, along with the tune NOEL, on pages 110–11. Both text and tune are in the public domain and may be reproduced without charge.

Order of Service

Great Holy One
spreading time and space,
show us who you are
in a human face.

The theme above is the refrain of the worship song "Great Holy One," from *We Can Be Messengers*, by Susan Heafield and Brian Wren (for words and music, see pp. 10 and 18). This quotation serves as the theme of the service, whether or not the song is sung.

Song of Preparation or Entrance Song: "Great Holy One," (Stanzas 1–3, Bridge, and Refrains)

"Welcome to All!" A Call to Worship
(Spoken by a worship leader or leaders)

> Welcome to all:
> happy or sad,
> rejoicing or grieving,
> seeking or believing.
> Welcome to all, here is good news:
> To you is born this day, in the city of David,
> a Savior, who is Christ the Lord.
> His name is Jesus, which means, "Liberator," "Rescuer,"
>   "Deliverer."
> His life changed the world.
> His living presence changes us today.
> Lift up your hearts. Rejoice! Give thanks to God!

Hymn: "Hark, the Herald Angels Sing!"
(AHB, AMNS, BP, CH, CH4, ELW, H82, NCH, PH, RJS, UMH, VU)

Prayer: "God of Peace"
(See p. 89.)

Lighting the Christ Candle—Year B
(Optional: See p. 52.)

Hymn: "Angels We Have Heard on High"
(BP, CH, ELW, H82, NCH, PH, MH, VU)
or "Angels from the Realms of Glory
(AHB, AMNS, BP, CH, CH4, ELW, H82, NCH, PH, RJS, UMH, VU)

Great, Holy One, Spreading Time and Space . . .

Introduction
(*Spoken by a worship leader or leaders*)

> Our theme is the verse quoted in our order of worship (OR: is
> the refrain of our Advent song):
>
> > Great Holy One, spreading time and space,
> > show us who you are, in a human face.
>
> Our first two readings tell of God, spreading time and space,
> and of ourselves, needing God, in a world gone wrong:

First Reading: God, Revealed in Creation (Acts 17:22–34a)
(*Spoken by one or more people*)

> The apostle Paul visits the Greek city of Athens,
> debates with philosophers,
> and proclaims the one true God.

> > "Athenians, I see how extremely religious you are in every
> >   way.
> > For as I went through the city
> > and looked carefully at the objects of your worship,
> > I found among them an altar with the inscription, 'To an
> >   unknown god.'
> > What therefore you worship as unknown, this I proclaim to
> >   you.
> > The God who made the world and everything in it, . . .
> > who is the ruler of heaven and earth,
> > does not live in shrines made by human hands,
> > [but is the universal giver of life and breath—indeed, of
> >   everything.]
> > God made all nations to inhabit the whole earth,
> > and allotted the times of their existence,
> > and the boundaries of the places where they would live,
> > so that they would search for God and perhaps grope for
> >   God and find God—
> > though indeed God is not far from each one of us.

For 'In God we live and move and have our being';
as even some of your own poets have said. . . .
Since we are God's offspring,
we ought not to think that the deity is like gold, or silver, or
    stone,
an image formed by the art and imagination of mortals.
While God has overlooked the times of human ignorance,
now God commands all people everywhere to repent,
because God has fixed a day on which God will have the
    world judged in righteousness
by a man whom God has appointed,
and of this God has given assurance to all by raising him
    from the dead."
When they heard of the resurrection of the dead, some
    scoffed;
but others said, "We will hear you again about this."
At that point Paul left them. But some joined him and be-
    came believers.

Here ends our reading.
Good Christian friends, rejoice!
Now ye need not fear the grave.
Jesus Christ was born to save!

Hymn: *"Good Christian Friends, Rejoice!"*
(And similar wordings; AHB, BP, CH, CH4, ELW, H82, NCH, PH, RJS, UMH, VU)
or "Behold the Great Creator Makes"
(AMNS)

Second Reading: *Rescuing a World Gone Wrong*
(Romans 7:14–25; 8:1–2)
(*Spoken by one or more people*)

The apostle Paul proclaims that we live in a world gone
    wrong,
where humankind has gone astray from God,
and we can't put ourselves right, or the world right,
even when we want to.

I do not understand my own actions.
For I do not do what I want,
but I do the very thing I hate.
Now if I do what I do not want,
I agree that God's law is good. . . .

I can will what is right, but I cannot do it.
For I do not do the good I want,
but the evil I do not want is what I do. . . .
So I find it to be a law that when I want to do what is good,
    evil lies close at hand.
For I delight in the law of God in my inmost self,
but I see in myself another law at war with the law of my
    mind, . . .
Wretched man that I am!
Who will rescue me from this body of death?
Thanks be to God through Jesus Christ our Lord!
There is therefore now no condemnation
for those who are in Christ Jesus.
For the law of the Spirit of life in Christ Jesus
has set you free from the law of sin and of death.

Here ends our reading.
Joy to the world, the Lord is come.
Let heaven and nature sing!
The living Christ can change the world
and break the curse of sin.
Thanks be to God!

Hymn: "Joy to the World"
(AHB, BP, CH, CH4, ELW, H82, NCH, PH, UMH, VU)
or "Long Ago, Prophets Knew"
(AHB, AMNS, BP)

Show Us Who You Are . . .

Introduction
(*Spoken by a worship leader or leaders*)

Long before Jesus was born, God's Holy Name was revealed to
    the people of Israel.
Today, Christians, Muslims, and Jews worship One God
but have different stories.
Our story as Christians is founded on the story of the Jews
because Jesus expressed
what his people already knew about God.
Our next three readings show us part of what they knew.

Third Reading: Compassionate and Forgiving (Psalm 103:1–12)

(Spoken by one or more people)

> Listen to an ancient song of praise
> that tells of God's unfailing love:

> Bless the Living God, O my soul,
> and all that is within me,
> bless God's holy name.

> Bless the living God, O my soul,
> and remember all God's benefits—
> who forgives all your iniquity,
> who heals all your diseases,
> who redeems your life from the Pit,
> who crowns you with steadfast love and mercy,
> who satisfies you with good as long as you live
> so that your youth is renewed like the eagle's.

> It is God who works vindication,
> and justice for all who are oppressed. . . .
> The Living God is merciful and gracious,
> slow to anger and abounding in steadfast love, . . .
> [and] does not deal with us according to our sins,
> nor repay us according to our iniquities.

> For as the heavens are high above the earth,
> so great is God's steadfast love
> to all who come with reverence;

> as far as the east is from the west,
> so far has God removed our transgressions from us.

> Here ends our reading.
> May the holy child of Bethlehem
> cast out our sin, enter in,
> and be born in us today.

Hymn: "O Little Town of Bethlehem"

(AHB, AMNS, BP, CH, CH4, ELW, H82, NCH, PH, RJS, UMH, VU)

Fourth Reading: Putting Wrongs Right (Psalm 146)

(*Spoken by one or more people*)

From the songs of ancient Israel,
we learn that God is not only awesome, but also active;
not neutral, but involved;
not a detached creator, but God among us,
longing to see justice done
and the humble lifted high:

Praise God, O my soul!
I will praise God as long as I live;
    I will sing praises to my God all my life long.

Do not put your trust in rulers,
    in mortals, in whom there is no help.
When their breath departs, they return to the earth;
    on that very day their plans perish.

Happy are those whose help is the God of Jacob,
    whose hope is in the Living God,
who made heaven and earth,
    the sea, and all that is in them;

who keeps faith forever;
    who executes justice for the oppressed;
    who gives food to the hungry.,
and sets the prisoners free;
    who opens the eyes of the blind,
[and] lifts up those who are bowed down;

God loves [those who do justice,]
[and] watches over the strangers;
    God upholds the orphan and the widow,
    but brings to ruin the way of the wicked.

Here ends our reading.
Let us pray, and work, and hope
for justice, kindness,
and "peace on earth, goodwill to all."

Hymn: "It Came upon the Midnight Clear"

(Here is my revision [see pp .102–3] and Arthur Sullivan's tune NOEL. Both are in public domain and can be reproduced free of charge. It may be advisable to teach text and tune during the weeks preceding this service.)

It came upon the midnight clear,
    that glorious song of old,
from angels bending near the earth
    to touch their harps of gold;
"Goodwill to all, and peace on earth:
    great news of joy we bring!"
The world in solemn stillness lay
    to hear the angels sing.

Still through the clouds of time they come
    with peaceful wings unfurled,
and still their heavenly music floats
    through all the weary world;
above its sad and lonely plains
    they bend on hovering wing,
and still, through all its babbled sounds,
    the blessed angels sing.

But with the woes of sin and strife
    the world has suffered long.
Beneath the angel-hymn have rolled
    two thousand years of wrong,
as warring armies clash and drown
    the love song that they bring;
O hush the noise of bomb and gun
    and hear the angels sing!

For still the days are hastening on
    by prophets seen of old,
when in our planet's circling years
    shall come a time foretold,
when peace shall over all the earth
    its newborn splendors fling,
as all the world sends back the song
    which now the angels sing.

Tune: NOEL
Traditional English Melody, arr. Arthur Sullivan, 1874
Poetic Meter: 8.6.8.6 D (Double Common Meter)

Fifth Reading: Working with Gentle Perseverance (Isaiah 42:1–4)
(Spoken by one or more people)

The prophet Isaiah proclaims God's chosen One,
whose gentle strength will put things right.

Here is my servant, whom I uphold,
   my chosen one, in whom I take delight!
I have put my spirit on him;
   he will establish justice among the nations.
He will not shout or raise his voice,
   or make himself heard in the street.
He will not break a crushed reed
   or snuff out a smoldering wick;
   unfailingly he will establish justice.
He will never falter or be crushed
   until he sets justice on earth,
   while coasts and islands await his teaching.

Here ends our reading.
May God give us the gentle strength of persevering love.

In a Human Face

Introduction
(Spoken by a worship leader or leaders)

We believe that in Jesus of Nazareth,
the Great Holy One, creator of the universe,
came to be with us, as one of us,
not just to be seen and touched and known,
but to do something, to make a difference:
to us and to the whole world.
So we shall hear how Jesus was born,
what kind of person he became,
and what his life reveals to us.

Sixth Reading: Born among Us (Luke 2:1–8 REB)
(Spoken by one or more people)

The Gospel of Luke tells how Jesus was born,
and who greeted him:

In those days a decree was issued by the emperor Augustus
for a census to be taken throughout the Roman world.
This was the first registration of its kind;
it took place when Quirinius was governor of Syria.
Everyone made their way to their own towns to be
    registered.
Joseph went up to Judea from the town of Nazareth in
    Galilee,
to register in the city of David called Bethlehem,
because he was of the house of David by descent;
and with him went Mary, his betrothed,
who was expecting her child.
While they were there the time came for her to have her
    baby,
and she gave birth to a son, her firstborn.
She wrapped him in swaddling clothes.
and laid him in a manger,
because there was no room for them at the inn.
Now in this same district there were shepherds out in the
    fields,
keeping watch through the night over their flock.

Here ends our reading.
Let us now sing the story of the shepherds, the angels,
and the glorious good news.

Hymn: "While Shepherds Watched"

(AHB, AMNS, BP, CH, CH4 ["While Humble Shepherds Watched "], H82, PH, RJS, UMH, VU)

or "Mimgxing canlan ye wei yang"

["Midnight Stars Make Bright the Skies"], (ELW)

"Hitsuji wa nemureri"

["Sheep Fast Asleep"], (NCH)

or "Pastores a Belén"

["As Shepherds Filled with Joy"], (NCH)

Seventh Reading: Teacher, Healer, Friend (Luke 13:10–17)

(Spoken by one or more people)

Here is a story from the Gospel of Luke.
It shows us what Jesus was like when he grew up:

[Jesus] was teaching in one of the synagogues on the
     sabbath.
And just then there appeared a woman
with a spirit that had crippled her for eighteen years.
She was bent over
and was quite unable to stand up straight.
When Jesus saw her, he called her over and said,
"Woman, you are set free from your ailment."
When he laid his hands on her,
immediately she stood up straight and began praising God.
But the leader of the synagogue,
indignant because Jesus had cured on the sabbath,
kept saying to the crowd,
"There are six days on which work ought to be done;
come on those days and be cured,
and not on the sabbath day."
But the Lord answered him and said,
"You hypocrites! Does not each of you on the sabbath
untie his ox or his donkey from the manger,
and lead it away to give it water?
And ought not this woman,
a daughter of Abraham
whom Satan bound for eighteen long years,
be set free from this bondage on the sabbath day?"
When he said this, all his opponents were put to shame;
and the entire crowd was rejoicing
at all the wonderful things that he was doing.

Here ends our reading.
Let us rejoice that God has come to us,
not with glamour, power, and wealth,
but through Jesus,
showing us God, with a human face.

Song: "Great Holy One" (Stanzas 4, 5, Bridge, and Refrains)

Eighth Reading: A Light for All Nations (Matthew 2:1–12)
(Spoken by one or more people)

Matthew tells how a group of wise seekers,
from a distant land and another religion,
come to greet the Christ Child,
as the light who shines for the entire world.

In the time of King Herod,
after Jesus was born in Bethlehem of Judea,
wise men from the East came to Jerusalem, asking,
"Where is the child who has been born king of the Jews?
For we observed his star at its rising,
and have come to pay him homage."

When King Herod heard this, he was frightened,
and all Jerusalem with him;
and calling together all the chief priests and scribes of the
        people,
he inquired of them where the Messiah was to be born.
They told him, "In Bethlehem of Judea;
for so it has been written by the prophet:
    'And you, Bethlehem, in the land of Judah,
        are by no means least among the rulers of Judah;
    for from you shall come a ruler
        who is to shepherd my people Israel.' "

Then Herod secretly called for the wise men
and learned from them the exact time when the star had
        appeared.
Then he sent them to Bethlehem, saying,
"Go and search diligently for the child;
and when you have found him, bring me word
so that I may also go and pay him homage."

When they had heard the king, they set out;
and there, ahead of them,
went the star that they had seen at its rising,
until it stopped over the place where the child was.

When they saw that the star had stopped,
they were overwhelmed with joy.
On entering the house, they saw the child with Mary his
        mother;
and they knelt down and paid him homage.
Then, opening their treasure chests,
they offered him gifts of gold, frankincense, and myrrh.
And having been warned in a dream not to return to
        Herod,
they left for their own country by another road.

Here ends our reading. Let us sing the story
of the seekers who followed a star.

Hymn: "The First Noel"
(AHB, BP, CH, CH4, ELW, H82, NCH, PH, UMH, VU)
or "As with Gladness Men of Old"
(AHB, AMNS, BP, CH, CH4, ELW, H82, NCH, PH, RJS, VU)
or "What Child Is This?"
(See pp. 87–88.)

Lighting of All Candles
(See p. 97.)

Hymn: "Silent Night"
(See p. 97.)

Petition: "Christ among Us"
(See p. 99.)

Ninth Reading: Seen, Heard, Touched, and Known
(1 John 1:1–4; John 1:10–18)
(*Spoken by one or more people*)

> In his first letter, and also in his Gospel,
> John shows us
> the meaning of Jesus' birth, life, death, and living presence:
>
> > We declare to you what was from the beginning,
> > what we have heard,
> > what we have seen with our eyes,
> > what we have looked at and touched with our hands,
> > concerning the word of life—
> > this life was revealed, and we have seen it and testify to it,
> > and declare to you the eternal life that was with the Father
> > and was revealed to us—
> >
> > we declare to you what we have seen and heard
> > so that you also may have fellowship with us;
> > and truly our fellowship is with the Father
> > and with his Son Jesus Christ.
> > We are writing these things so that our joy may be
> >   complete.

[For] the Word became flesh and lived among us,
and we have seen his glory,
the glory as of a father's only son,
full of grace and truth.

No one has ever seen God.
It is God the only Son,
who is close to the Father's heart,
who has made God known.

Here ends our reading.
O come let us adore him, Christ the Lord!
Blow out your candles now,
but take the light of Christ with you
out into the world.

(Main lights are switched on. Candles are extinguished.)

Hymn: "O Come, All Ye Faithful"
(AHB, AMNS, BP, CH, CH4, ELW, H82, NCH, PH, UM, VU)

Blessing
(See p. 100.)

CHAPTER 7

What If God Was One of Us?

A CHRISTMAS SERVICE OF SCRIPTURE AND SONG

(YEAR C)

This service can be used in any year.
For lectionary users, the appropriate year is specified.

Order of Service

Voices of Hope—An Optional Vocal "Prelude" [1]

(Spoken by different voices, recorded or live, with or without supporting musical improvisation)

You shall know that I am in the midst of Israel,
and that I, the Living God, am your God and there is no other.
And my people shall never again be put to shame.

The Living God has taken away the judgments against you,
and has turned away your enemies.
The Living God is in your midst;
you shall fear disaster no more.
The Living God will rejoice over you with gladness,
renew you with love,
and exult over you with loud singing.

I myself will search for my sheep, and will seek them out.
I myself will be the shepherd of my sheep,
and I will make them lie down.
I will seek the lost, and I will bring back the strayed.
I will bind up the injured, and I will strengthen the weak.
I will feed them with justice.

I will make a covenant of peace with them.
My dwelling place shall be with them;
and I will be their God, and they shall be my people.

I will return to Zion, and will dwell in the midst of Jerusalem;
Jerusalem shall be called the faithful city.
Old men and old women shall again sit in the streets of
        Jerusalem,
And the city shall be full of boys and girls playing in its streets.
They shall be my people and I will be their God,
in faithfulness and in righteousness.

Sing and rejoice, O daughter Zion!
For see, I will come and dwell in your midst.
Many nations shall join themselves to me on that day,

---

1. Quoted or adapted from Joel 2:27; Zephaniah 3:15, 17; Ezekiel 34:11–16; 37:26–27; Zechariah 8:3–8; 2:10; Isaiah 12:6.

and shall be my people; and I will dwell in your midst.
Shout aloud and sing for joy, O royal Zion,
for great in your midst is the Holy One of Israel.

Song of Preparation or Entrance Song: "Rejoice, Give Thanks, for God Is near Us" (chorus, verse 1, chorus)
(See pp. 11, 22)

"We Meet to Worship God," a Call to Worship
(Spoken by a worship leader or leaders)

> We meet to worship God,
> and to give thanks for the birth of Jesus,
> who lived, and died, and rose from death
> to show that God loves us,
> that God calls us,
> and that God is with us.

"Come to Us Today," a Gathering Prayer
(Spoken by a worship leader or in unison)

> Living Christ, come to us today.
> If we are hurt, heal us.
> If we have run away, bring us home.
> If we are trapped or lost, rescue us.
> Bring us together and touch our hearts,
> that we may know you, love you, and follow you,
> today, tomorrow, and always.
> We ask it in your name. Amen.

Hymn: "Joy to the World"
(AHB, BP, CH, CH4, ELW, H82, NCH, PH, RJS, UMH, VU)
or "Long Ago, Prophets Knew"
(AHB, AMNS, BP)

Lighting the Christ Candle Year C
(Optional: See p. 71.)

Song: "Rejoice, Give Thanks" (chorus only)

Hymn: "From Heaven Above to Earth I Come"
(AHB, CH, ELW, H82, NCH, PH, RJS, VU)
or "In the Bleak Mid-Winter"
(AMNS, BP, CH4, ELW, H82, NCH, PH, RJS, UMH, VU)
or "Infant Holy, Infant Lowly"
(AHB, BP, CH, ELW, PH, RJS, UMH, VU)
or "Unto Us a Boy Is Born"
(AHB, BP, CH4, H82, RJS, VU)

Up in Heaven All Alone?

Introduction
(*Spoken by a worship leader or leaders*)

In January 1996, Joan Osborne's recording of Eric Bazilian's song "One of Us" was one of the top ten hits in the United States.

The song asks a series of simple but deep questions:
Does God have a name?
And if God had a name,
would you say it if you met God in glory, face to face?

What would God look like if God had a face?
And if seeing God's face meant you had to believe in Jesus and the saints,
would you still want to see?

Yes, says the singer, God is great and God is good,
but—and here's the insistent question in the refrain:

What if God was one of us
just a slob like one of us
just a stranger on the bus
trying to make his way home
back up to heaven all alone,
nobody calling on the phone
except for the pope maybe in Rome?[2]

It may be tempting to dismiss this portrait of God and say, "That's not true. God is with us! It's Christmas! Rejoice!"

---

2. Words and music by Eric Bazilian. © 1995 Human Boy Music. All rights administered by WB Music Corp. All rights reserved. Used by permission of Alfred Publishing Co., Inc.

But suppose that, for many people, the song does ring true?

Suppose God seems good perhaps, yet distant and powerless,
unable to quench the world's violence or ease its suffering?
Suppose this is the way some of us feel, sometimes, even if we
      don't say so?

If we take the song seriously,
yet tell a more hopeful story,
our story may perhaps be heard as good news
if we tell it modestly, not triumphantly,
and if we can show that we live by it.

First Reading: The Awesome Starmaker Loves Us (Psalm 8 REB)
(Spoken by one or more people)

For thousands of years,
people have looked at the stars
not hidden by a haze of city lights
but blazing bright in darkness
and have realized how immense the universe must be.

Even when people thought the earth was flat,
they knew that the heavens were beyond us.

Yet the people of Israel also testify
that God is not removed from us,
up in heaven all alone,
but loves us and cares about us.
Here is one of the hymns they sang:

> Living God, Sovereign Love,
>   how majestic is your name in all the earth!
> You have set your glory above the heavens.
>   Out of the mouths of babies and infants
> you have built a fortress against your foes,
>   to silence the enemy and the avenger.

> When I look at your heavens, the work of your fingers,
>   the moon and the stars that you have established;
> what are human beings that you are mindful of them,
>   mortals that you care for them?
> Yet you have made them a little lower than God,
>   and crowned them with glory and honor.

You have given them dominion over the works of your
    hands;
    you have put all things under their feet,
all sheep and oxen,
    and also the beasts of the field,
the birds of the air, and the fish of the sea,
    whatever passes along the paths of the seas.

Living God, Sovereign Love
    how majestic is your name in all the earth!

This is the end of our reading.
Let us praise God, far beyond us,
who loves us and cares for us,
and let us be ready
to live the faith we sing.

Hymn: "See amid the Winter's Snow"
(BP, PH, RJS, VU)
or "Once in Royal David's City"
(AHB, AMNS, BP, CH, CH4, ELW, H82, NCH, PH, RJS, UMH, VU)

Introduction and Second Reading: God—Hidden, Near, or Both? (Voices from Psalm 10 and Psalm 46)

(For a worship leader [A] and two people or groups of voices [B and C], speaking from different places. The reading is enhanced if they stand and face each other, provided they project well or have microphones. The bidding ["The Living God is with us"] and the response printed in bold are spoken by the worship leader and the congregation; they may be printed, projected on-screen, or learned by ear.)

A   In the first and largest part of the Christian Bible, many voices
from ancient Israel give their testimony about God. The
primary witness is that God loves us and is with us. But
sometimes God is hidden or absent—a stranger, up in heaven,
not necessarily all alone but certainly out of reach. The
greatness of the Bible is that both positive and negative voices
have permission to be heard. Here are two contrasting voices,
from Psalm 10 and Psalm 46.

A   The Living God is with us.
    The God of Jacob is our refuge.

B   Why, O God, do you stand far off?
    Why do you hide yourself in times of trouble?

For the wicked boast of the desires of their heart,
 those greedy for gain curse and renounce you.
In their pride they say, "God will not seek it out";
 all their thoughts are, "There is no God."

C God is our refuge and strength,
  always ready to help
in times of trouble.
Therefore we will not fear,
though the earth should change,
 though the mountains shake in the heart of the sea.

A The Living God is with us;
The God of Jacob is our refuge.

B Why do the wicked renounce God,
  and say in their hearts, "You will not call us to account?"
They seize the poor and drag them off in their net.
They think in their heart, "God has forgotten.
God will never see it."

C Come, see what the Living God has done:
who makes wars cease to the end of the earth;
who breaks the arrows, shatters the spear,
and burns the shields of warriors.
"Be still, and know that I am God!
I am exalted among the nations,
I am exalted in the earth."

A The Living God is with us;
The God of Jacob is our refuge.

B O God, lift up your hand;
do not forget the oppressed.
Do justice for the orphan and the oppressed,
so that those from earth may strike terror no more.
     (Ps. 10:1, 3–4, 12, 9c, 11, and 18,* interwoven
       with Ps. 46:1–2, 7, 8ac, 9, and 11*)

A This is the end of our reading.
Give thanks to God
and pray that we may reach out to the world,
speaking honestly about the hiddenness of God
yet trusting that God is with us.

Hymn: "O Come, O Come, Emmanuel"

(AHB, AMNS, BP, CH, CH4, ELW, H82, NCH, PH, RJS, UMH, VU)

(*Sing complete hymn or selected stanzas.*)

Introduction and Third Reading: What Kind of God Is with Us? (Micah 3:9–12; 6:8)

(*Spoken by one or more people*)

> From ancient Israel to modern Judaism
> and from Judaism into Christianity
> comes this unbroken witness:
> God is Holy. God is Unique. God is One.
> And God takes the initiative.
>
> In major events like the exodus from Egypt
> and through inspired voices called "prophets,"
> it is God who—as it were—keeps calling us on the phone,
> not the other way round.
>
> God creates. God chooses. God calls. God loves.
> And therefore also, "God is with us."
>
> But the prophets knew and proclaimed
> that if the people did not keep God's covenant,
> "God is with us!" was as empty as "God bless us!"
> The prophet Micah makes this clear
> and asks a persistent question:
>
> > Your rulers give judgment for a bribe,
> > your priests teach for a price,
> > your prophets give oracles for money;
> > yet they lean upon the Holy Name and say,
> > "Surely God is with us!"
> > And so, because of you,
> > Jerusalem will be plowed under
> > and left in ruins.
>
> For what does the Holy Name require of you:
> Only this—
> > to do justice, and to love kindness,
> > and to walk humbly with your God?

(*Mic. 3:11–12 and 6:8**)

This is the end of our reading.
Let us show the world that we believe God is with us
by doing justice, loving kindness,
and walking humbly with God.

Hymn: "What Does the Lord Require of You?"
(STRATHDEE; AHB, BP, CH, VU)
or "What Does the Lord Require?"
(BAYLY; AHB, AMNS, BP, CH, H82, PH, UMH)
or "For the Healing of the Nations"
(AMNS, BP, CH, CH4, ELW, NCH, PH, RJS, UMH, VU)
or "God of Grace and God of Glory"
(AHB, AMNS, BP, CH, ELW, H82, RJS, UMH, VU)
or "Hail to the Lord's Anointed"
(AHB, AMNS, BP, CH, CH4, ELW, H82, NCH, RJS, UMH, VU)

Fourth Reading: "Emmanuel—God with Us" (Matthew 1:18–25)
(*Spoken by one or more people*)

What if God was one of us?
Not watching from a distance,
but taking the risks
and having the inside knowledge
of being born, being human,
living and facing death?
This is the good news of Christmas.
Listen to how Matthew tells it:

This is how the birth of Jesus Christ came about.
His mother Mary was betrothed to Joseph;
before their marriage she found she was going to have a
child
through the Holy Spirit.
Being a man of principle,
and at the same time wanting to save her from exposure,
Joseph made up his mind to have the marriage contract
quietly set aside.
He had resolved on this,
when an angel of the Living God appeared to him in a
dream and said,

"Joseph, son of David, do not be afraid to take Mary home
with you to be your wife.

It is through the Holy Spirit that she has conceived.
She will bear a son; and you shall give him the name Jesus
(which means "Liberator")
for he will save his people from their sins."

All this happened in order to fulfill what the Living God
    declared through the prophet:
"A virgin will conceive and bear a son, and he shall be called
    Emmanuel,"
a name which means "God is with us."
When he woke, Joseph did as the angel had directed him;
he took Mary home to be his wife, . . .
and when her son was born,
he named the child Jesus.   (*REB**)

This is the end of our reading.
Give thanks to God,
who came to be one of us,
with a body, a mind, a language, and a name. Amen.

Hymn:"The Angel Gabriel from Heaven Came"
(AHB, BP, CH4, ELW, H82, PH, RJS)
or "What Child Is This?"
(See above p. 87)
or "While Shepherds Watched"
AHB, AMNS, BP, CH, CH4 ["WHILE HUMBLE SHEPHERDS WATCHED THEIR FLOCKS"],
H82, PH, RJS, UMH, VU)

Fifth Reading: God's Promise Fulfilled
(Selections from Luke 2:32–40)
(Spoken by one or more people)

Every one of us, and everyone on earth,
is born into a particular time, a particular place,
a particular language and tradition.
It is the only way of being human.
So when we hear these particulars about Jesus
in the second chapter of Luke's Gospel,
we know that he was indeed one of us:

Eight days later the time came to circumcise him,
and he was given the name Jesus,
the name given by the angel before he was conceived.

Then, after the purification had been completed, . . .
they brought him up to Jerusalem to present him
      to God. . . .

There was at that time in Jerusalem a man called Simeon
who was upright and devout,
and watched and waited for the restoration of Israel. . . .
It had been revealed to him by the Holy Spirit
that he would not see death until he had seen the Lord's
      Messiah.
Guided by the Spirit he came into the temple;
and when the parents brought in the child Jesus, . . .
Simeon took him in his arms, praised God, and said:

"Now, Lord, you are releasing your servant in peace,
according to your promise.
For I have seen with my own eyes the deliverance
you have made ready in full view of all nations:
a light that will bring revelation to the Gentiles
and glory to your people Israel."

There was also a prophet, Anna the daughter of Phanuel,
of the tribe of Asher.
She was a very old woman,
who had lived seven years with her husband after she was
      first married,
and then alone as a widow to the age of eighty-four.
She never left the temple, but worshiped night and day
      with fasting and prayer.
Coming up at that very moment, she gave thanks to God;
and she talked about the child
to all who were looking for the liberation of Jerusalem.

When they had done everything prescribed in the law, . . .
they returned to Galilee. . . .
The child grew big and strong and full of wisdom;
and God's favor was upon him. (*Luke 2:21–32, 36–40 REB**)

This is the end of our reading.
Give thanks to God:
who came to be one of us
as one of God's chosen people,
in a particular place and time.

Hymn: "Angels We Have Heard on High"
(BP, CH, ELW, H82, NCH, PH, UMH, VU)
or "Angels from the Realms of Glory"
(AHB, AMNS, BP, CH, CH4, ELW, H82, NCH, PH, RJS, UMH, VU)

Sixth Reading: Foreigners Follow Their Star (Matthew 2:1–12)

(Spoken by one, two, or more people. Note: According to Matthew the wise men reach Jerusalem two years after Jesus' birth [Matt. 2:1, 16]. They kneel to a toddler, not at a manger!)

The child called "God Saves" and "God with us"
soon attracted attention
from visitors wanting to honor him
and from a tyrant seeking to destroy him.
Listen to the story, in Matthew, chapter 2:

> In the time of King Herod,
> after Jesus was born in Bethlehem or Judea,
> wise men from the East came to Jerusalem, asking,
>
> "Where is the child who has been born king of the Jews?
> For we observed his star at its rising,
> and have come to pay him homage."
>
> When King Herod heard this, he was frightened,
> and all Jerusalem with him;
> and calling together all the chief priests and scribes of the
>   people,
> he inquired of them where the Messiah was to be born.
> They told him,
>
> "In Bethlehem of Judea;
> for so it has been written by the prophet."
>
> Then Herod secretly called for the wise men
> and learned from them the exact time when the star had
>   appeared.
> He sent them to Bethlehem, saying,
>
> "Go and search diligently for the child;
> and when you have found him,
> bring me word so that I can also go and pay him homage."

. . . They set out; and there, ahead of them,
went the star that they had seen at its rising,
until it stopped over the place where the child was.
When they saw that the star had stopped,
they were overwhelmed with joy.

On entering the house,
they saw the child with Mary his mother;
and they knelt down and paid him homage.
Then, opening their treasure chests,
they offered him gifts of gold, frankincense, and myrrh.

Later they were warned in a dream not to return to Herod,
so they left for their own country by another road.

This is the end of our reading.
Give thanks to God, who took the risk
of being truly one of us.

Song: "Rejoice, Give Thanks, for God Is near Us" (chorus, verse 2, chorus)

(See pp. 11–13.)

or Hymn: "The First Noel"

(AHB, BP, CH, CH4, ELW, H82, NCH, PH, UMH, VU)

or "As with Gladness Men of Old"

(AHB, AMNS, BP, CH, CH4, ELW, H82, NCH, PH, RJS, VU)

Seventh Reading: Despised and Rejected (Luke 2:33–35 and Isaiah 53:2–3, 5)

(Spoken by one or more people)

In the song refrain with which we began, the line "just a slob
     like one of us"
seems to have a slightly self-mocking tone.
It suggests that the singer and her peers,
or human beings in general,
are average, ordinary, and unappealing.
More often the word "slob" is an insult,
a term of abuse for someone who is coarse, lazy, dirty, or rude.
Our sources tell us that the adult Jesus
was a controversial prophet,
loved by many
but also insulted and abused,

treated as worse than a slob, and that his suffering was
>   foreseen by Simeon
when his parents brought their infant son to the Temple:

> The child's father and mother were full of wonder
> at what was being said about him.
> Simeon blessed them and said to Mary his mother,
> "This child is destined to be a sign that will be rejected;
> and you too will be pierced to the heart.
> Many in Israel will stand or fall because of him;
> and so the secret thoughts of many will be laid bare."
>> (*Luke 2:33–35 REB*)

In the prophecy of Isaiah we hear these words:
> He had no form or majesty that we should look at him,
>> nothing in his appearance that we should desire him.
> He was despised and rejected by others;
>> a man of suffering and acquainted with infirmity;
> and as one from whom others hide their faces
>> he was despised, and we held him of no account.
> . . . .
> But he was wounded for our transgressions,
>> crushed for our iniquities;
> upon him was the punishment that made us whole,
>> and by his bruises we are healed.
>> (*Isa. 53:2–3, 5*)

New Hymn: "Christ, You Did Not Sit with God"[3] (*Philippians 2:5–11*)

POETIC METER: 7.7.7.7.

(*Suitable tunes include CANTERBURY, MONKLAND, ORIENTIS PARTIBUS, SAVANNAH, and SONG 13. The aim is simplicity, a hymn that children and adults can sing.*)

> Christ, you did not sit with God,
> grabbing all the power you could,
> but instead gave all you had
> for our glory and our good.
>
> Taking off your shining robe,
> leaving everything but love,
> taking "Jesus" as your name,
> born as one of us you came.

3. Brian Wren. Copyright © 2007 by Hope Publishing Company for the USA, Canada, Australia, and New Zealand, and by Stainer and Bell for all other territories. All rights reserved. Used by permission.

Strong in love, you chose to live
like a servant or a slave,
teaching, showing God to us,
tortured, dying on a cross.

Jesus Christ, your praise we sing.
Help us give you everything.
On your way we'll follow you.
Guide and govern all we do.

God With Us Always, in Christ (Optional Dramatized Meditation)

(Use either Bob McGee's chorus, "Emmanuel," if you have legal access to it, or use the verse that follows.)

Immanuel, we meet you now,
in human flesh and bone,
the Word and Wisdom of our God
as power in weakness shown.[4]

(Suitable tunes include DETROIT, DUNDEE, KILMARNOCK, IRISH, MARTYRDOM, RICHMOND, ST. FULBERT, ST. MAGNUS, ST. PETER, TALLIS'S ORDINAL, THIS ENDRIS NYGHT, WILTSHIRE, and WINCHESTER OLD. If feasible, use pictures, projected images, and/or dramatic tableaux as suggested or indicated below. You will need a large cross or someone who stands in the shape of a cross. "Emmanuel" [McGee] or "Immanuel, We Meet You Now" [Wren] is sung by all or by a choir or soloist[s].)

Introduction and Commentary

(Spoken by one or more people)

In the Gospel of Matthew, chapter 1, verse 23, we read;

Look, the virgin shall conceive, and bear a son,
and they shall name him "Emmanuel,"
which means, "God is with us."

We shall sing a simple chorus based on these words.

(OR: Bob McGee has given us a simple yet profound chorus based on these words. [Sing the chorus chosen.])

---

4. Brian Wren. Copyright © 2007 by Hope Publishing Company for the USA, Canada, Australia, and New Zealand, and by Stainer & Bell for all other territories. All rights reserved. Used by permission. Poetic Meter: 8.6.8.6. (Common Meter).

Imagine first the infant Jesus,
newly born,
fed by Mary,
cradled by Joseph,
and sing with quiet joy–

(Someone mimes cradling an infant as the chosen chorus is sung gently, as a lullaby.)

Imagine Jesus grown up,
teaching about God's love,
eating with outcasts,
and healing a leper with a word,
and sing with praise—

(One or more people mime or pantomime[5] being welcomed and healed as the chosen chorus is sung. Then someone points to a cross, to a projected image of a cross, or to a person facing away from the congregation and standing with outstretched arms. Hold the gesture as the following lines are spoken and the chosen chorus is sung.)

Imagine Jesus betrayed,
arrested, crucified,
facing death with courage,
for God and for us,
and sing—

(The chosen chorus is sung.)

Imagine Jesus Christ,
in Easter light,
risen from the dead,
alive for ever,
and meeting his disciples:

(Someone speaks the words above and then moves to where Scripture readers have stood and without introduction gives the Eighth Reading.)

Eighth Reading: Christ Is with Us, So Tell the World (Matthew 28:16–20)

Now the eleven disciples went to Galilee,
to the mountain to which Jesus had directed them. . . .
And Jesus came and said to them,
"All authority in heaven and on earth has been given to me.
Go therefore and make disciples of all nations,
baptizing them in the name of the Father
and of the Son and of the Holy Spirit,

---

5. By "mime" I mean a series of silent gestures. By "pantomime" I mean a gesture or tableau that is made and then held during what is spoken or sung.

and teaching them to obey everything I have commanded
you.
And remember,
I am with you always, to the end of the age."

(*Matt. 28:16–20*)

(*Joyfully sing the chorus chosen.*)

Song: "Rejoice, Give Thanks" (complete song)
(See above pp. 11–13.)
and/or Hymn: "Away in a Manger"
AHB, BP, CH, CH4, ELW, H82, NCH, PH, RJS, UMH, VU)
or "Good Christian Friends, Rejoice!"
(AND SIMILAR WORDINGS; AHB, BP, CH, C4, ELW, H82, NCH, PH, RJS, UMH, VU)
or "Behold the Great Creator Makes"
(AMNS)

Lighting of All Candles
(*See p. 69.*)

"Because of Jesus," A Call to Praise
(*Spoken by worship leader after candles have been lit and other lights turned off*)

> Because of Jesus,
> we know that God takes notice of us,
> God cares about us day by day,
> God loves us, calls us,
> and is always with us.
> Sing it with your lips,
> and believe it in your hearts,
> as Christ the Savior is born.

Hymn: "Silent Night"
(*See pp. 97–98.*)

Ninth Reading: Nothing Can Separate Us from God's Love (Romans 8:35–39)
(*Spoken by three voices—A, B, and C*)

> A   Out of suffering and hardship,
>   Paul celebrates the good news
>   that in Jesus Christ, God is with us always:

B	What will separate us from the love of Christ?
C	Will hardship?
A	or distress?
B	or persecution?
C	or famine?
A	or nakedness?
B	or peril?
C	or sword?
ABC together	No, in all these things we are more than conquerors through Christ who loved us.
C	For I am convinced that neither death,
B	nor life,
A	nor angels,
C	nor rulers,
B	nor things present,
A	nor things to come,
C	nor the forces of the universe,
B	nor the highest things,
A	nor the lowest things,
C	nor anything else in all creation—
ABC together	Nothing, nothing at all can ever separate us from the love of God in Christ Jesus our Lord.
A	And so God was one of us,
B	flesh and bone, like one of us,
C	not a stranger on a bus,
B	but our Savior on a cross,
A	bringing us home.
ABC together	**Amen.**

(Main lights are turned on. Candles are extinguished.)

Hymn: "O Come, All Ye Faithful"
(AHB, AMNS, BP, CH, CH4, ELW, H82, NCH, PH, RJS, UMH, VU)

Blessing
(See p. 100.)

CHAPTER 8

Worship Resources for Christmastide

(YEARS A, B, AND C)

This chapter contains resources for
Christmas Eve, Christmas Day,
and any other suitable time in the Christmas season.

Four Christmas Hymns by Brian Wren

Worship is enriched when hymns are treated as poems and read aloud as such. Thus the hymns in this section can be spoken as poems, sung by soloist(s) or choir, or sung by a congregation. Anyone who legally has this book may speak these poems aloud from it. To access the music and obtain permission to *reproduce* words or music, follow the copyright information on p. ix.

Good Is the Flesh[1]

POETIC METER: 10.10.10.10.10. DACTYLIC

Good is the flesh that the Word has become,
   good is the birthing, the milk in the breast,
   good is the feeding, caressing, and rest,
   good is the body for knowing the world,
Good is the flesh that the Word has become.

Good is the body for knowing the world,
   sensing the sunlight, the tug of the ground,
   feeling, perceiving, within and around,
   good is the body, from cradle to grave,
Good is the flesh that the Word has become.

Good is the body, from cradle to grave,
   growing and aging, arousing, impaired,
   happy in clothing, or lovingly bared,
   good is the pleasure of God in our flesh,
Good is the flesh that the Word has become.

Good is the pleasure of God in our flesh,
   longing in all, as in Jesus, to dwell,
   glad of embracing, and tasting, and smell,
   good is the body, for good and for God,
Good is the flesh that the Word has become.

1. Brian Wren. Copyright © 1989 Hope Publishing Company for the USA, Canada, Australia, and New Zealand, and by Stainer & Bell Limited for all other territories. All rights reserved. Reprinted by permission.

Hail, Undiminished Love[2]

POETIC METER: 6.7.6.7.

Hail, undiminished love,
destroyed, yet resurrected,
foreshadowed and foreseen,
yet always unexpected.

Through old, familiar forms,
in weekly repetition,
God startles us with grace,
yet makes no imposition.

Exotic angel hosts
can show us nothing stranger
than pregnancy and birth,
and parents at a manger.

No Scripture, star, or sign
can guarantee the Savior.
A child, a man, a life
are all there is on offer.

He calls us to decide—
for love, or domination,
for tenderness, or pride,
for justice, or oppression.

Hail, unexpected love
in old, familiar story.
This ordinary birth
is Christ, the hope of glory!

2. Brian Wren. Copyright © 1986, 1996 by Hope Publishing Company for the USA, Canada, Australia, and New Zealand, and by Stainer & Bell for all other territories. All rights reserved. Used by permission.

Her Baby, Newly Breathing [3]

POETIC METER: 8.7.8.7. D

Her baby, newly breathing,
with wailing, needful cry,
by Mary kissed and cradled,
is lulled in lullaby.
Long months of hope and waiting,
the thrill and fear of birth,
are crowned with exultation,
and God is on the earth.

The eyes that gaze at Mary
have yet to name or trace
the world of shape and color,
or recognize a face;
yet Holiness Eternal
is perfectly expressed
in hands that clutch unthinking,
and lips that tug the breast.

The milk of life is flowing
as Mary guides and feeds
her wordless Word, embodied
in infant joys and needs.
Enormous, formless strivings,
and yearnings deep and wide,
becradled in communion,
are fed and satisfied.

How mother-like the Wisdom
that carried and gave birth
to all things, seen and unseen,
and nurtured infant earth—
unstinting, unprotected,
prepared for nail and thorn,
constricted into maleness,
and of a woman born.

3. Brian Wren. Copyright © 1989 by Hope Publishing Company for the USA, Canada, Australia, and New Zealand and Stainer & Bell Limited for all other territories. All rights reserved. Used by permission.

When a Baby in Your Arms[4]

When a baby in your arms
grips your little finger tight,
   but cannot tell you why,
   or say your name,
remember Christmas,
   a shining star above,
   and tiny fingers,
   clutching from the cradle,
holding you with love, eternal love.

When a baby in your arms
   gives a yelling, bawling cry
   that wails a nameless need
   you can't ignore,
remember Christmas,
   a shining star above,
   and hear the crying,
   crying from the cradle,
calling you with love, eternal love.

When a baby in your arms
   gazes deep into your eyes,
   and you're the only face
   that baby knows,
remember Christmas,
   a shining star above,
   and eyes a-gazing,
   gazing from the cradle,
meeting you with love, eternal love.

4. Brian Wren. Copyright © 1993 by Hope Publishing Company for the USA, Australia, Canada, and New Zealand, and by Stainer &
Bell for all other territories. All rights reserved. Used by permission.

Worship Elements for Christmastide

RCL READINGS ARE THE SAME IN ALL THREE YEARS.
CHRISTMAS EVE: ISAIAH 9:2–7; PSALM 96; TITUS 2:11–14; LUKE 2:1–14 (15–20)
CHRISTMAS DAY DAWN: ISAIAH 62:6–12; PSALM 97; TITUS 3:4–7; LUKE 2:(1–7) 8–20
CHRISTMAS DAY: ISAIAH 52:7–10; PSALM 98; HEBREWS 1:1–4 (5–12); JOHN 1:1–14

Give Thanks for the Birth of Jesus

A Call to Worship

(Spoken by a worship leader or leaders)

> We meet to worship God,
> and to give thanks for the birth of Jesus,
> who lived, and died, and rose from death
> to show that God loves us,
> God calls us,
> and God is with us.
> Bring mind and body, heart and voice:
> Our Savior comes. Rejoice! Rejoice!

The Grace of God Has Appeared

A Call to Worship from Titus 2:11–14 and Hosea 12:6

(Spoken by a worship leader or leaders, or by worship leader[s] and the congregation. The responding or congregation voice is in bold.)

> The grace of God has appeared,
> bringing salvation to all,
> **training us to renounce godless ways**
> **and worldly desires,**
> **and in the present age to live a life**
> **that is self-controlled, upright, and godly,**
> **while we wait for the blessed hope**
> **and the manifestation of the glory**
> **of our God and Savior, Jesus Christ.**
>
> Jesus Christ sacrificed himself for us
> to set us free from wickedness.
> **Therefore let us ask God's help**
> **to turn our lives around,**
> **maintain loyalty and justice,**
> **and wait continually for our God.**

A Great Light

A Call to Worship from Isaiah 9:2–7 and Psalm 96

(Spoken responsively between leader[s] and congregation, with the congregation speaking the parts in bold type; or spoken antiphonally between two voices or groups of voices. For the latter, two halves of the congregation may stand and face each other; groups of voices may speak antiphonally from the sides of the worship space; or choir and congregation may speak antiphonally.)

Sing to the Living God! Sing a new song!
Sing to God, all the earth!
The people who walked in darkness
have seen a great light.
On those who lived in a land as dark as death
a light has dawned.
The boots of tramping warriors
and soldiers' coats rolled in blood
shall be burned as fuel for the fire.
For a child has been born for us,
a son given to us.
Authority rests upon his shoulders;
and he is named
Wonderful Counselor, Mighty God,
Everlasting Father, Prince of Peace.
Let the heavens be glad, let the earth rejoice.
Let the sea roar, and all that fills it.
Let the field exult, and everything in it.
Let the trees of the forest sing for joy.
For the Living God is coming,
coming to judge the earth,
to judge the world with righteousness,
and the peoples with truth.

The Goodness and Loving-kindness of God[5]

A Call to Worship drawn from Titus 3:4–7

(Spoken by a worship leader or leaders, worship leader[s] and choir, or worship leader[s] and congregation. The responding or congregation voice is printed in bold.)

Friends, here are words we can trust:
"The goodness and loving-kindness of God our Savior
has dawned upon the world.
Christ is born. Christ has died. Christ is risen. Hallelujah!

---

5. Also suitable for Easter and throughout the year.

Through the water of rebirth,
and the renewing power of the Holy Spirit,
God has saved us, not for any good deeds of our own,
but because God is merciful.
Christ is born. Christ has died. Christ is risen. Hallelujah!
God has poured out the Holy Spirit upon us
through Jesus Christ our Savior
so that, having been justified by God's grace,
we might in hope become heirs to eternal life.
Christ is born. Christ has died. Christ is risen. Hallelujah!"
These are words we can trust.
Let us worship God.

How Beautiful upon the Mountains

A Call to Worship or Call to Prayer from Isaiah 52:7–10
and Luke 2:9–14

(Spoken by a worship leader or leaders, worship leader[s] and choir, or worship leader[s] and congregation. The responding or congregation voice is printed in bold.)

Look and see
how beautiful upon the mountains
are the feet of the messenger who announces peace,
who brings good news,
who announces deliverance,
who says to Zion, "Your God reigns!"
Here is good news of great joy to all people:
To us is born today, in the city of David,
a Savior, the Life-Giver, the Messiah.
Open your ears and listen.
The sentinels lift up their voices,
together they sing for joy.
Glory to God in highest heaven,
and on earth peace,
to all in whom God delights.

Why Have We Come?[6]

A Dramatized Meditation for Worship

(After the introduction, a series of voices is heard. The speakers can be visible in or around the congregation [standing as they speak, to be easily heard] or the voices can be prerecorded and played over a sound system. Change the word today if appropriate [e.g., tonight, this morning, etc.]. Accompany the voices by pictures and images if available.)

Introduction

(Spoken by a worship leader)

> In the name of Jesus Christ, welcome to worship.
> None of us knows all the stories, all the reasons
> why we have come here today,
> but we can guess at some of them
> and declare that everyone is welcome.
> Here are some of our guesses,
> spoken by different voices:

> "I come because I always come. I couldn't be anywhere else.
> This is where my heart is, in familiar faces, memories, songs,
> and prayers. I know it all so well, but sometimes it surprises
> me. So I come, expecting familiarity, but ready to be
> surprised."

> "I am surprised—surprised to be here. I don't trust the
> church, any church. Churches say they follow Jesus, but they
> don't do what Jesus did. And yet, somehow, today, I'm giving it
> one more chance. Is God really here? Show me."

(Spoken by two voices, A and B)

> A   I grew up here.
> B   I used to worship here.
> A   For most of the year, I am somewhere else.
> B   But today is a day when I need to reconnect—with this place,
>   this group of people . . .
> A   . . . with memories, our dreams and hopes, our longings.
> B   Don't judge us because we don't come more often. Shouldn't
>   you welcome strangers?

> "I'm getting to know you in this church. You seem to have
> your ups and downs, and your fair share of arguments,
> mistakes, and hurt feelings. And yet, something real is

6. For Advent, Christmas, Easter, and other great days in the year.

happening here—God, the Spirit, Jesus, or whatever. I'm here because I am hungry and thirsty for love, for hope, for God."

(Spoken by three voices, C, D, and E)

C We are people whose lives have been shaken
D by tragedy and crisis;
E by sadness, loss, and grief;
C by failure and disappointment;
D by pain we cannot talk about;
E by worries about family, children, work, unemployment—you name it.
C We're hoping for something good today.
D We want some relief from the pressure.
E We long for peace and hope.

"I know why I am here. Every other day of the week I'm treated as if I don't matter. I am put down or shut out. Here I am welcomed and respected. I am somebody. I am a child of God. And everybody here knows it, too."

"I don't know why I have come. Does it matter? Do I really need to explain? I'm here! I've come!"

Friends, whatever the reason that you've come,
we declare and hope to show
that you are welcome,
and we hope that everyone will know
that God is real and God is here.
Let us pray:

No Empty Words

A Collect

(Spoken by a worship leader or in unison)

Holy God,
remove from us now
empty words, idle words,
and hollow deeds.
Fill our worship with the Spirit of truth,
that we may know that you are real,
that you are here,
and we are yours,
through Jesus Christ. Amen.

Christ Child, Bringer of Joy

A Prayer of Adoration

(Spoken by a worship leader or in unison)

Christ Child, bringer of joy
and bearer of good news,
we praise and adore you
for you have comforted your people
and set them free;
and all the ends of the earth
shall see your salvation.
We praise and adore you. Amen.

Welcome, Mary's Child

A Litany of Praise and Adoration from Luke 2:1–20

(Spoken responsively by two voices or by worship leader[s] and congregation. The responding or congregation voice is printed in bold. Speak or sing the bidding and response.)

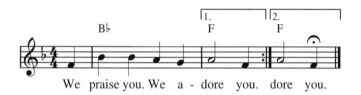

We praise you. We a - dore you. dore you.

Welcome, Mary's child,
born away from home
at the end of a journey.
We praise you. **We adore you.**

Welcome to an occupied territory
where your birthplace is decreed
by an empire's tax demand.
We praise you. **We adore you.**

Welcome, newborn Christ,
wrapped in a mother's care
sleeping in a feeding trough.
We praise you. **We adore you.**

Welcome to a town
with no-one to greet you
but shepherds, called unclean.
We praise you. **We adore you.**

Welcome Mary's child,
prophet, healer, teacher,
friend and sovereign leader,
yesterday, today, for ever.
We praise you. **We adore you.**
Amen.

Active Expression of Divinity

A Prayer of Praise from Hebrews 1:1–13

(Spoken by a worship leader or leaders)

Living Christ,
energetic Word,
active expression of Divinity,
we praise you
for everything you said and did
to demonstrate God's glory:

for your parables, encounters, and healings,
your proclamation of good news to the poor
and your hosting of a welcome table
where no-one is excluded or unclean.

And most all we praise you
for removing the stain of sin
and making us clean for ever
by going to the cross
and taking us with you
into the presence of God.

Living Christ,
offspring of holiness
and reflection of divinity,
we praise you, we thank you, we love you,
now and for ever. Amen.

Plan A or Plan B?

A Meditative Prayer about Incarnation

(Spoken by a worship leader or leaders)

> God, did you decide to become human
> only because the human race
> had gone so badly wrong?
> Was the birth of Christ, as it were, Plan B?
>
> Or was it Plan A?
> Did you always plan to come,
> whatever happened?
> Would you have come to a good world
> where most of the time we loved our neighbors
> and kept your laws?
>
> Or did you come because
> our world is full of violence and despair
> and only you can make it right?
>
> God, our wondering is not disrespect
> but a way of saying, "Wow!" and "Thank you!"
> because the true wonder is,
> the wonderful truth is,
> that you did come,
>
> and that your Word became flesh, and lived among us,
> full of grace and truth.
>
> No one has ever seen you,
> but your offspring, your child, your Chosen one,
> the One who is closest to your heart
> has made you known.
> We thank you. We praise you. We love you. We adore you.
> And with your help, we will follow you.
> Amen.

Never Grasped or Defeated[7]

A Petition from John 1:4–8

(Spoken by a worship leader or in unison)

---

7. For Christmas Eve/Day or the Second Sunday after Christmas in Years A, B, and C.

Christ among us, light of the world,
you are never grasped or defeated
by the darkness within and around us.
Shine upon us, and among us,
and make your worldwide church
a chandelier of diversity,
as it gleams and sparkles
in endless reflections of your love.
We ask it in your name. Amen.

The Word Became Flesh, Our Flesh[8]

A Thanksgiving and Petition on Embodiment and Sexuality—
from John 1:14 and Genesis 1:27–28, 31

(Plain and italic type denote "East" and "West," which are two halves of the congregation, preferably facing each other. Bold type is for parts spoken by all. The introduction is spoken by one or more voices. The hymn "Good is the Flesh" (see p. 137) can be spoken or sung in conjunction with this prayer.)

Introduction

God made human beings in the divine image and likeness,
male and female together.
And when everything had been created,
God saw that it was very good.
The Word became flesh and lived among us,
full of grace and truth.
Therefore let us give thanks and ask for healing:

EAST For the goodness of our bodies,
and because the Word became flesh, our flesh,

We will be glad and sing a new song.

WEST *For families, friends, and strangers,*
and for human beings,
young and old, of every kind,
because they are made—body, mind, and spirit—
in the image of God,

We will be glad and sing a new song.

EAST That we may know our bodies as sacred
and as temples of the Holy Spirit,

8. For Christmas Eve/Day, the Second Sunday after Christmas in Years A, B, and C, or other suitable occasion.

Holy God, heal us.

WEST   *That we may know the loveliness and beauty*
of our own body, and of every body,

Holy God, heal us.

EAST   For all whose body-self is hurt and violated,
by unwanted touch or by physical force,

Holy God, hear our prayer.

WEST   *For all whose bodies are hurt and abused*
by cruel words and pornographic pictures,
and by rape, torture, and war,

Holy God, hear our prayer.

EAST   That we may recover the unity
of mind, body, and spirit,

WEST   *And that we may present our whole selves,*
soul and body, as a living sacrifice to God,
which is our spiritual worship,

Holy God, hear our prayer. Amen

Confidence to Pray

A Petition on Persistence in Prayer from Isaiah 62:6b–7

(See also Luke 18:1–8.)

Call to Prayer
(Spoken by a worship leader)

The prophecy of Isaiah declares,

"You who remind the Living God,
take no rest, and give God no rest,
until God establishes Jerusalem
and makes it renowned throughout the earth."
Let us pray.

Prayer

(Spoken by a worship leader or in unison)

> God of promise and hope,
> calling us to be your people,
> give us confidence to pray
> and persistence in prayer
> to remind you of your promises to us
> and remind ourselves
> of our promises to you,
> in Jesus Christ. Amen.

We Know That God Takes Notice

An Affirmation of Faith

(*Spoken by a worship leader or leaders*)

> Because of Jesus,
> we know that God takes notice of us,
> cares about us day by day,
> loves us, calls us,
> and is always with us.
> Sing it with your lips,
> and believe it in your heart,
> as Christ the Savior is born.

Alive with Us, Alive in God [9]

A Litany of Praise and Adoration Celebrating the Life and Work of Jesus Christ

(*Spoken responsively by two voices or by worship leader[s] and congregation. The bidding and echoed response are printed in bold and should be spoken or sung.*)

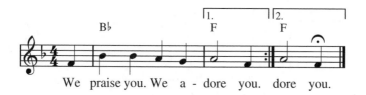

9. For Christmas and any time of year.

Living Christ, risen from the dead,
alive with us, alive in God:
We praise and adore you—
    we praise and adore you.

Because you did not cling to equality with God
but humbled yourself and became a human being:
We praise and adore you—
    we praise and adore you.

Because like us you were formed in the womb,
delivered, nursed, and protected:
We praise and adore you—
    we praise and adore you.

Because you were born
not in a haven of tranquillity
but on a journey ordered by an empire
to count and tax its subjects:
We praise and adore you—
    we praise and adore you.

Because you were schooled and raised
not in a warlord's fortress,
an emperor's palace,
or a millionaire's mansion,
but in a low-status household
with little to offer except faith, hope, and love:
We praise and adore you—
    we praise and adore you.

Because you gave yourself entirely to God
and proclaimed God's justice and love
consistently and with courage:
We praise and adore you—
    we praise and adore you.

Because you gave your life for us
and suffered torture and humiliation,
and because you trusted in God
even when forsaken:
We praise and adore you—
    we praise and adore you.

Living Christ, born of Mary,
crucified and risen,
alive in us, alive in God:
We praise and adore you—
    we praise and adore you. Amen.

To Convince Us of Your Love

A Pastoral Prayer

(Spoken by a worship leader or leaders—use it in whole or in part, as spoken prayer only or as a visual meditation with video, mime, banners, or still images.)

God of love, lover of creation,
lover of all humankind,
we praise and adore you.

You are the source of our life.
You have created us to know you and love you,
and today we praise and thank you
for all the ways you have taken
to convince us of your love.

Thank you, God,
for the signs of your love
in the workings of the universe,
and in the faiths of humankind.

Thank you, above all,
that you humbled yourself to be one of us
to convince us of your love.

Thank you for everything that Jesus said and did
to show what a human life can be
when you are fully in it—
from birth to death, from cradle to cross.

Thank you, that before we knew you,
while we were yet sinners,
resisting your law and your love,
Christ died for us.

Thank you that Jesus, like us,
did not come from nowhere
but from a family, a tradition, and a people
where you were loved and known.

Thank you, also, for people and traditions
that have shaped us, loved us,
made us what we are
and tried to give us confidence to love.

We confess with sorrow
that in spite of everything you have done
to convince us of your love,
we resist you so strongly, so deeply.

Dismantle our resistance to your love.
Melt the ice of our distrust.
Turn us toward you and each other.
Help us to put you first
in all our decisions.
Make us trustworthy, faithful, and true.

With the confidence that you love us and cherish us,
we pray for others whom you love.

We pray for the people of your first, unbroken covenant,
through whom Jesus came—
for Jewish people everywhere.
We praise you for their resistance and resilience
in the face of persecution and hatred,
especially from Christians.
We praise you for every Jew
who treasures Torah, does justice,
loves kindness, and walks humbly in your love.
Protect and guide the people of your first, continuing
      covenant,
and fill them with your Spirit.

Make a just and peaceful future
for Christian and Jew,
and shape a just and peaceful future
for Israelis and Palestinians
in the land of your ancient promise.

We pray also for the other people of the Book,
who love and follow your truth
revealed through the prophet Muhammad.
Move us to pray together, listen to each other's stories,
and walk in the way of peace.

We pray for Buddhists, Hindus, for atheists and agnostics,
for people of all religions,
and for people who name the name of Christ
in ways we cannot accept as true.

Forgive our sins against you and against each other.
Cleanse the polluted streams of pride and hate
in us, in this land,
and in every part of the world (especially . . .).

We pray for all who have been so hurt, oppressed, or abused
that they cannot believe they are lovable
or trust in other people's love.
Give them hope and heal their wounds.
Give patience, wisdom, and skill
to social workers, health workers, teachers, and volunteers
who try to prevent abuse and to build trust
as agents of community care.

We pray for your church throughout the world
and for this congregation.
Make every church a safe and trustworthy community
where people can rely on one another
and grow in faith and love.
Protect us against breaches of trust
and every kind of abuse.

We pray for our world.
Curb the violence that springs from failure to love
and destroys love and trust.
Build love and respect for every person—child or adult,
man or woman, old or young,
of every sexual orientation
and every ethnic identity.
Hear our prayers for particular people who need love and
        care, (especially . . .).

Living God, draw together our prayers, silent and spoken,
as we show our trust in your love
by joining all your church
in the prayer of Jesus: Our Father . . .

Go, Holding in Your Heart

A Christmastide Dismissal

(Spoken by a worship leader or leaders)

> Go, holding in your heart
> the child Mary waited for,
> the child you once were,
> and the children you know or have known.

Among, Before, and Beside

A Trinitarian Blessing

(Spoken by a worship leader or leaders, for any time of year or following the Christmastide Dismissal above)

> May the peace of the Origin of All,
> the peace of Christ, crucified and risen,
> and the peace of the Spirit, One God,
> be among you, to connect you,
> and before you, to lead you,
> and beside you, to guide you,
> now and for ever. Amen.

Go Out through the Gates

A Charge and Blessing from Isaiah 62:10

(Spoken by a worship leader or leaders)

> Go out, go out through the gates.
> Prepare a way for the people.
> Build up, build up a highway
> and clear it of stones.
> Hoist a signal to all earth's peoples.
> Proclaim the Living God's deliverance
> to earth's farthest bounds.
> And may the Living God strengthen, protect, and guide you,
> now and for ever. Amen.

CHAPTER 9

Worship Elements for the First Two Sundays after Christmas

(YEARS A, B, AND C)

Including a Short Communion Service

First Sunday after Christmas: Year A

RCL READINGS: ISAIAH 63:7–9; PSALM 148; HEBREWS 2:10–18; MATTHEW 2:13–23

Praise the Holy Name[1]

A Call to Worship from Psalm 148 and Isaiah 63:7–9

(Spoken by a worship leader or leaders, or by worship leader[s] and congregation. The responding or congregation voice is in bold.)

Praise the living God!
Praise God from the heavens:
Sun and moon, and shining stars,
praise the living God!

Praise the Holy Name,
whose word speaks all things into being,
who created the forces of the universe
and the laughter of children.
Praise the Holy Name!

Praise the Living God from the earth:
clouds and storms and ocean currents,
fish in the sea and creatures of the deep,
animals and cattle, insects and birds,
praise the living God!

People and rulers,
powerless and power brokers,
young women, young men,
children and elders together,
praise the Holy Name!

Praise the living God,
whose Name alone is exalted,
our Rescuer and Deliverer
in all our distress.
Praise the living God!

Praise the Holy Name
who did not rely only on angels and messengers

---

1. Also suitable for the First Sunday after Christmas Day, Years B and C, and the Fifth Sunday of Easter, Year C.

but came among us in person,
whose living presence saves us!
Praise God's Holy Name!

Face to Face, as a Person

A Call to Worship Based on Isaiah 63:7–9

(Spoken by a worship leader)

We meet here today
to declare the praiseworthy acts of the living God,
for God has come among us
not through an angel or a messenger
but face to face, as a person,
with an abundance of steadfast love.
Welcome, then, in the name of Jesus Christ,
Mary's child, healer and teacher,
Savior and Friend. Amen.

Infant Christ, Star of Hope

A Collect in Response to Matthew 2:1–2 and 2:16–18

(Spoken by a worship leader or in unison. For other prayers prompted by Matthew 2, see the materials for Epiphany on pp. 198–99.)

Infant Christ, star of hope,
whose light brought seekers of wisdom
and murderers with swords,
shine among us, here and now,
that seekers may be touched by your presence
and agents of hate may meet, in us,
forgiving, persistent peace
in your name. Amen.

Agent of God's Perfection

Praise and Petition from Hebrews 2:10–18

(Spoken by a worship leader or leaders, or by worship leader[s] and congregation. The responding or congregation voice is printed in bold.)

Living Christ, agent of God's perfection,
pioneer of our salvation,
we praise you.

You revealed the mystery of God to us
by sharing our flesh and blood.

You bore the agony of execution
to free us from the fear of death.

Raised from death,
you give us the dignity and joy
of being your sisters and brothers.

Deliver us from the fear of death
and the deadly powers of this world
that we may follow your path,
die without fear,
and meet you in glory.
We ask it in your name.

Priest and Minister of God

A Collect from Hebrews 2:10–18

(Spoken by a worship leader or in unison)

Jesus of Nazareth,
priest and minister of God,
in every temptation and test
you proved yourself faithful and merciful.
Take us by the hand and lead us
when we are tested or enticed
so that we may stay faithful
and be merciful
in your name.

First Sunday after Christmas: Year B

RCL READINGS: ISAIAH 61:10–62:3; PSALM 148; GALATIANS 4:4–7; LUKE 2:22–40

Praise the Holy Name

A Call to Worship from Psalm 148 and Isaiah 63:8–9

(*See p. 158.*)

Called by a New Name

A Call to Worship from Isaiah 61:10-62:3

(*Spoken by a worship leader or leaders, or by worship leader[s] and congregation. The responding or congregation voice is in bold.*)

> Rejoice, rejoice in the One Holy Name!
> **Our whole being shall exult in God,**
> **who has clothed us with garments of salvation**
> **and covered us with robes of righteousness.**
> You shall be called by a new name
> that the mouth of the Living God will give.
> For as the earth brings forth its shoots
> and a garden causes what is sown in it to spring up,
> **so the great Holy Name**
> **will cause righteousness and praise**
> **to spring up before all the nations.**

More Faithful than Any Human Parent

A Collect Based on Galatians 4:4–7

(*Spoken by a worship leader or in unison*)

> Holy God, more compassionate and faithful
> than any human parent,
> any human child,
> move us in our close relationships
> so to imitate your ways
> that in failure, hurt, and harm,
> we may repent, forgive, and be forgiven
> through Jesus Christ. Amen.

By God's Generous Love

An Affirmation Prompted by Galatians 4:4–7

(Spoken by a worship leader or leaders, or by worship leader[s] and congregation. Use in whole or in part. The responding or congregation voice is printed in bold. All sing the response if it is sung. If it is spoken, all can say, "We are your daughters/sons," or women and men can each say what applies to them.)

We are your daugh - ters.   We are your sons.

We are your daugh - ters.   We are your sons.

By God's generous love in Jesus Christ,
we have been adopted as God's children,
members together of the household of God.

Whatever we do or say,
whatever others do or say,
we are God's beloved children:
We are your daughters.
We are your sons.

In want or wealth,
in sickness and health,
we are God's beloved children:
We are your daughters.
We are your sons.

When our loveliness is decried
and our gifts are denied,
we are God's beloved children:
We are your daughters.
We are your sons.

When we heed God's call or run away,
when we walk with God or hide from God,

we are God's beloved children:
We are your daughters.
We are your sons.

Through failure, success, fulfillment, and loss,
we are God's beloved children:
We are your daughters.
We are your sons.

In the heights of joy and the depths of shame,
we are God's beloved children:
We are your daughters.
We are your sons.

In ignorance and awareness, awakening and repentance,
we are God's beloved children:
We are your daughters.
We are your sons.

Through all our life
and beyond our death,
we are God's beloved children:
We are your daughters.
We are your sons.

Thanks be to God!
Amen!

To Praise Your Promise and Presence

A Collect from Luke 2:22–40

(Spoken by a worship leader or in unison)

Holy God, Holy Spirit,
you inspired Anna and Simeon in their old age
to praise your promise and presence
in the infant Jesus.
Inspire us as we grow older
to recognize your presence
and nourish your gifts
in children, infants, and youth,
that we may praise you together
in Jesus Christ. Amen.

The Wisdom of a Child

A Collect Prompted by Luke 2:22–40

(Spoken by a worship leader or in unison)

Wisdom of God,
playful and profound,
patiently persuasive,
gentle and strong,
reveal yourself to us
in the faith of girls and boys
that we may respectfully receive
the wisdom of a child
and give you praise. Amen.

Let the Little Children Come

A Collect Prompted by Luke 2:22–40 in Light of Mark 10:14

(Spoken by a worship leader or in unison)

Welcoming Christ, still you tell us,
"Let the little children come to me; do not stop them."
Make our churches and homes
safe and welcoming spaces,
where all without exception
may meet and trust your love.
We ask it in your name. Amen.

For People of Any Age

A Thanksgiving Prompted by Luke 2:22–40

(Spoken by a worship leader or in unison)

Thank you, God,
for people of any age
whose faith is not eroded by doubt,
broken by adversity,
or soured by cynicism.
Thank you, God,
for everyone
whose faith revives our spirits,
warms our hearts,
and renews our hopes
in Jesus Christ. Amen.

First Sunday after Christmas: Year C

RCL READINGS: 1 SAMUEL 2:18–20, 26; PSALM 148; COLOSSIANS 3:12–17; LUKE 2:41–52

(For "Praise the Holy Name," A Call to Worship from Psalm 148 and Isaiah 63: 8–9, see the First Sunday after Christmas in RCL Year A on pp. 158–59.)

Word Become Human

A Call to Worship Drawn from Colossians 3:5–11 (which comes before today's RCL reading) and from the RCL reading, Colossians 3:12–17)

(Spoken by a worship leader or leaders, or by worship leader[s] and congregation. The responding or congregation voice is printed in bold.)

We meet to worship God, whose Word has become human
and is born among us.
Amen! Alleluia!
From the cradle, the cross, and the empty tomb, Christ calls
us, saying,
**Put to death your worldly ways: fornication, evil desire, and
greed;**
lying, anger, malice, and all abusive words and deeds.
These are the ways we once followed, when we were living the
unredeemed life.
**But now, in Christ, we have stripped off the old self with its
practices.**
We have clothed ourselves with the new self
that is being renewed in the image of its creator.
In that renewal there is no division between Gentile and Jew,
female and male, slave and free,
for Christ is breaking all barriers—
of age and gender,
orientation, color and class.
Amen! Alleluia!

Prayers Drawn from Colossians 3:12–15

(Spoken by a worship leader or in unison)

Christ Our Mother

A Petition

Christ our mother,
who bore the pain of death
to give us second birth,
shape and stitch for us
the clothes of compassion, kindness, humility, patience, and
          love
and make them such a perfect fit
so that we become what we wear,
in your name. Amen.

Rule Us with Your Peace

A Collect

(Spoken by a worship leader or in unison)

Christ, alive among us,
as we draw near to you,
and embrace, bump, and bruise one another,
rule us with your peace
so that, clothed in love,
we may bear with one another,
forgive as we have been forgiven,
and be thankful
in your name. Amen.

Whatever We Do

A Litany of Praise from Colossians 3:12–17

(Spoken responsively by two voices or by worship leader[s] and congregation. The responding or congregation voice is in bold. The bidding and response are the same phrase, uttered and then echoed. Speak or sing the bidding and response.)

With grate - ful hearts we will sing   to God!

Dear friends, let us promise one another,
that whatever we do, in word or deed,
we will do everything in the name of Christ Jesus,
through whom we give thanks to the God of love,
Author of the Word made flesh,
mother and father and maker of all:
With grateful hearts
we will sing to God!

Beloved children of God
As God's chosen ones, holy and beloved,
with grateful hearts
we will sing to God!

Bearing with one another, if anyone has a complaint,
with grateful hearts
we will sing to God!

Clothed in love and governed by the peace of Christ,
with grateful hearts
we will sing to God!

Teaching and learning from one another,
admonishing and supporting one another,
with grateful hearts
we will sing to God!

Bound by the freedom of Christ,
whose word dwells richly among us,
with grateful hearts
we will sing to God!
Amen!

Jesus, Faithful Jew

A Litany of Praise Drawn from Luke 2:41–52

(Spoken responsively by two voices or by worship leader[s] and congregation. The responding or congregation voice is in bold. The bidding and response are the same phrase, uttered and then echoed. Use a chime or small bell [CH] as a cue to say or sing the bidding and response.)

Je - sus, faith-ful Jew,   we praise you, we   praise you.

Jesus of Nazareth, born among us,
crucified and risen,
we remember with gratitude
the parents who raised you,
the traditions that formed you,
and the faith in which you lived and died:
(CH)   **Jesus, faithful Jew,
we praise you.**

Going with your family to Jerusalem,
standing in the Temple courtyard,
hearing the chanting of psalms,
smelling the smoke of sacrifice:
(CH)   **Jesus, faithful Jew,
we praise you.**

Schooled in the practice of your faith,
knowing from an early age
that God is Holy, Unique, and One,
and that you belonged by birth
to God's own chosen people:
(CH)   **Jesus, faithful Jew,
we praise you.**

Sharing in the Passover meal,
hearing and telling the story
of slavery, deliverance, and covenant;
learning to love Adonai God
with heart and soul and mind and strength,
and your neighbor as yourself:
(CH)   **Jesus, faithful Jew,
we praise you.**

Learning and doing Torah,
learning of Moses and Elijah;
David, Ruth, and Deborah;
chanting the words of the prophets,
sitting among the teachers,
asking and answering questions:
(CH)   **Jesus, faithful Jew,
we praise you.**

Puzzling your anxious parents
by speaking of God's holy Temple
as your Father's house,
and honoring your father and mother
by accepting their loving authority
as you grew in wisdom and years:

(*CH*) **Jesus, faithful Jew,
we praise you.**

Asking and Answering Questions

A Collect from Luke 2:41–52

(Spoken by a worship leader or in unison)

Youthful Jesus,
sitting among the teachers,
asking and answering questions;
by your Spirit move us
to ask the deep questions of faith,
that we may grow in the asking,
in your name. Amen.

Second Sunday after Christmas, Years A, B and C

RCL READINGS: JEREMIAH 31:7–14; PSALM 147:12–20; EPHESIANS 1:3–14; JOHN 1:(1–9) 10–18

I Shall Gather a Great Company

A Call to Worship or Affirmation of Faith Drawn from Jeremiah 31:7–14

(Spoken by a worship leader or leaders, or by worship leader[s] and congregation. The responding or congregation voice is in bold.)

Thus says the One Holy Name—
See, I shall gather a great company
from the farthest parts of the earth,
and they shall proclaim, give praise, and say,
The One Holy Name
is our Deliverer, our Shepherd,
our Mother and our Father!
Amen! Hallelujah!

The One Holy Name
gathers old and young
in every condition:
sightless and seeing,
leaping and limping,
hearing and hearing impaired—
and they shall proclaim, give praise, and say,
The One Holy Name
is our Deliverer, our Shepherd,
our Mother and our Father!
Amen! Hallelujah!

With weeping they shall come,
and with consolations I will lead them back.
I will let them walk by brooks of water,
in a straight path in which they shall not stumble;
and they shall proclaim, give praise, and say,
The One Holy Name
is our Deliverer, our Shepherd,
our Mother and our Father!
Amen! Hallelujah!

Their life shall become like a watered garden,
and they shall never languish again.
Then shall the women rejoice in the dance,
and old men and young shall be merry.
I will turn their mourning into joy,
and give them gladness for sorrow,
and they shall proclaim, give praise, and say,
The One Holy Name
is our Deliverer, our Shepherd,
our Mother and our Father!
Amen! Hallelujah!

God Alone, through Jesus Christ!

An Act of Praise Based on Ephesians 1:3–14

(Spoken by a worship leader or leaders, or by worship leader[s] and congregation. Bidding and response are the phrase printed in bold, spoken and then echoed or sung.)

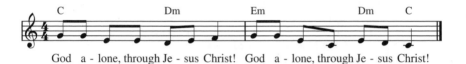

God a - lone, through Je - sus Christ! God a - lone, through Je - sus Christ!

Dear Friends, consider these questions:

Who chose us in Christ before space and time were conceived,
before the universe exploded into immensity?
God alone, through Jesus Christ!

Who destined us for adoption as beloved children,
to be holy and blameless in God's presence?
God alone, through Jesus Christ!

Who has paid off all our debts and purchased our redemption
through the shedding of Christ's blood on the cross?
God alone, through Jesus Christ!

Who can mend the harm we have done,
the hurt we have inflicted,
and the wrongs we cannot put right?
God alone, through Jesus Christ!

Who can forgive all our trespasses,

our sin against God
and against our neighbors?
God alone, through Jesus Christ!

To whom do we owe our love, loyalty,
thanksgiving, and praise?
God alone, through Jesus Christ!

Who has lavished grace upon us,
and plans in the fullness of time
  to bring all things to completion?
God alone, through Jesus Christ!
Amen!

The End of Killing

A Collect Prompted by Ephesians 1:7

(Spoken by a worship leader or in unison)

Risen Christ,
whose blood was shed,
not to satisfy God's needs
but to show God's love,
guide us so to tell the story of your cross
that it proclaims the end of killing
and the beginning of loving
in your name. Amen.

Prayers in a Trinitarian Framework and Other Worship Materials for Christmas, the Second Sunday after Christmas, Trinity Sunday, and Anytime

Introductory Note

As devout Jews, the first followers of Jesus-Messiah knew and passionately believed that God is Holy, Unique, and One. No other gods must be allowed to get in the way of the One. All other objects of worship are idols. Jews could not compromise on this primary article of faith (Deut. 6:4). Many were prepared to die for it and did so.

Yet from very early on, the followers of Jesus-Messiah had three experiences of the One. Christian Scripture (the New Testament) has many examples of this threefold pattern (see Matt. 10:16–20; 12:15–21; 28:16–19; Mark 1:9–13; Luke 4:16–21; 10:21–22; John 20:19b–22; Acts 1:6–8; 2:14–24, 32–33, 37–39; 7:54–56; 10:34–43; 10:44–48; 20:22–28; Rom. 5:1–8; 8:14–17, 26–30; 15:14–19, 30; 1 Cor. 12:1–3; 2 Cor. 13:13; Gal. 4:4–7; Eph. 3:14–19; 4:1–6; 2 Thess. 2:13–14; Titus 3:4–8; Heb. 9:11–14; 1 Pet. 1:1–2; 1 John 4:13–16).

Through centuries of debate and controversy, Christian faith arrived at the conviction that this threefold experience could not truthfully be collapsed into sameness nor divided into separateness. So every attempt to speak about or to the "Holy One, Holy Three" (as recent Lutheran worship resources helpfully express it) is misleading even when helpful. Trinity speech tends either toward sameness (e.g., "The Author [who speaks the] Word [thus giving out] Breath," which in human speech means one person doing three things), or separateness (e.g., Augustine's "Lover, Beloved, and Energy of Loving," which in human speech means two people and the elusive bond between them). The classic way of speaking ("Father, Son, and Holy Spirit") carries the weight of tradition from the Bible and creeds and is technically accurate, if you are at home in its technicalities. It does, however, fit snugly into patriarchal society and is all too easily heard—in the words of one critic—as an all-male, one-parent family with a whoosh of vapor.

Because John's Gospel stands at the beginning of Christian thinking about these matters, it is "pre-Trinitarian." The resources below offer both classic and more expansive language for the Three who are One.

You Do Not Return Empty

A Litany of Praise from Isaiah 55:11; John 1:1–14; and other parts of John's Gospel (e.g., 4:34; 5:30; 17:4; 20:21), using NRSV and REB.

(The bidding [in italics] and response [in bold] are spoken or sung by a worship leader and congregation responsively or by two worship leaders. They may be printed or projected or announced and practiced before the prayer begins.)

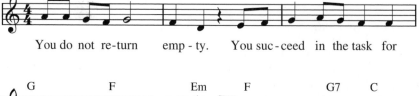

You do not re-turn   emp - ty.   You suc - ceed   in the task   for

which you were sent. Hal - le - lu - jah! Hal - le - lu - jah!

Living Word of God,
before the beginning, you were.
You were in God's presence,
and all that God is, you are.
You accomplish God's purpose.
You do not return empty.
You succeed in the task for which you were sent.
Hallelujah!

You became flesh and lived among us,
and we have seen your glory,
like the glory of a beloved child/the Father's only Son,
full of grace and truth.
You accomplish God's purpose.
You do not return empty.
You succeed in the task for which you were sent.
Hallelujah!

The works that God gave you to complete
bear witness to the One who sent you.

You accomplish God's purpose.
You do not return empty.
You succeed in the task for which you were sent.
Hallelujah!

You glorified God on earth
by finishing the work God gave you to do.
Uplifted on a Roman cross,
you draw all people to yourself
and accomplish God's purpose.
You do not return empty.
You succeed in the task for which you were sent.
Hallelujah!

Crucified, tortured to death,
glorified by God and honored by all your people,
you cry out, "It is accomplished,"
and give up your spirit.
You do not return empty.
You succeed in the task for which you were sent.
Hallelujah!

Raised from death, you greet your disciples,
saying, "Peace be with you.
As the One who lives sent me, so I send you/As the Father
    sends me, so I send you."
You breathe on us and say,
"Receive the Holy Spirit!"
You do not return empty.
You succeed in the task for which you were sent.
Hallelujah!

Name above All Names

A Trinitarian Litany of Praise

(Use in whole or in part. The bidding [in italics] and response [in bold] are spoken or sung by a worship leader and congregation responsively or sung by all. They should be announced and practiced before the prayer begins.)

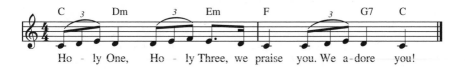

Great Name above all names,
You alone are God—Holy, Unique, and One.
Everything else we idolize, everyone else we worship
is a denial, a distraction, and a disappointment,
a false trail and a false hope.
Great Name above all names,
Spirit, Son, and Father,
Holy One, Holy Three,
we praise you! We adore you!

Never wrapped up in your own mystery,
but endlessly and always
dancing your inclusive dance:
sending, seeking, saving:
Great Name above all names,
Lover, Beloved, and Energy of Love,
Holy One, Holy Three,
we praise you! We adore you!

Life-giving Word, forever spoken and sent,
creating all things,
you are beyond the farthest galaxies
yet closer than our heartbeat.
You became flesh for us
to overcome the powers of death.
In union with the Author and the Breath,
you create, sustain, and redeem.
Holy One, Holy Three,
we praise you! We adore you!

Life-giving Father,
neither female nor male,
source and origin of everything,
always you reach out in love
to reconcile us to you and each other
and bring us eternal life.
In union with the Spirit and the Son,
you redeem, create, and sustain.
Holy One, Holy Three,
we praise you! We adore you!

Energy of love, Life-giving Spirit,
flowing out from the Lover and the Beloved,
you fill the universe

and all living things.
You bring us together in Christ
and breathe through every culture and belief.
In union with the Lover and the Beloved,
you sustain, create, and redeem.
Holy One, Holy Three,
we praise you! We adore you!

Great Name above all names,
you are the Author who speaks the Word
and in speaking gives out the Breath.
You are the Lover embracing the Beloved
and expressing the Energy of love.
You are the Son born from the Father,
together pouring out the Spirit.
Holy One, Holy Three,
we praise you! We adore you!
Amen.

A Short Communion Service with a Trinitarian Prayer of Thanksgiving

Words of Institution (Mark's Gospel)
(Spoken by a worship leader or leaders)

In the Gospel of Mark, chapter 14
we hear that on the night when Jesus was betrayed to the
        governing authorities,
he had supper with his disciples.
    While they were eating, he took a loaf of bread,
    and after blessing it, he broke it, gave it to them, and said,
    "Take; this is my body."
    Then he took a cup, and after giving thanks he gave it to
        them,
    and all of them drank from it.
    He said to them, "This is my blood of the covenant,
    which is poured out for many."

(*Mark 14:22–24*)

By doing this, Jesus declared that from his death,
God would bring new life, new hope,
and new creation.

Invitation to the Table

Through Jesus, we know that God knows us,
cherishes us, and loves us.
Through Jesus we believe and trust
that God is faithful and true.

Come to this table,
not because you must
but because you may;
not because you are worthy
but because you are hungry;
not because you are ready
but because you are thirsty.
Come, because Christ invites us,
saying,
    I am the bread of life.

Whoever comes to me will never be hungry.
Whoever believes in me will never be thirsty.
Whoever comes to me I will never drive away.

(*John 6:35, 37b*)

As Jesus took bread and wine
and gave thanks before sharing it,
so we also give thanks to God.

Prayer of Thanksgiving

(Spoken by a worship leader or leaders, or by worship leader[s] and congregation. The responding or congregation voice is printed in bold. This does not need to be printed. Announce the call and response and practice it once: "With all our heart **we praise you and thank you.**")

Holy One, Holy Three—Spirit, Son, and Father,
you unfolded time and space
and created us to love and be loved,
to live on this earth, and tend to it for your glory.
With all our heart
we praise you and thank you.

Holy One, Holy Three—Author, Word, and Breath,
you chose your covenant people
and revealed yourself as holy, incomparable, and elusive—
as liberator, judge, and compassionate, forgiving love.
With all our heart
we praise you and thank you.

Holy One, Holy Three—Lover, Beloved, and Energy of Love,
you became human in Jesus,
whose love goes beyond our limits,
reaching out to good and bad alike
and calling us to practice peace, mercy, and kindness;
to forgive as we have been forgiven;
and to love even our enemies.
With all our heart
we praise you and thank you.

Holy One, Holy Three—Giver, Given, and Gifting,
as we share this bread and cup,
we remember how Jesus died for us,
bore our sins in his body on the tree,
defeated the powers of this age,
and lives among us here and now,

breaking our dividing walls
and giving us good news.
With all our heart
we praise you and thank you.

Holy Spirit, power and presence of Holy Three, Holy One,
make this bread and cup
our communion in the body and blood of Christ.
With all our heart
we praise you and thank you.

With all your people
we join together,
using our own language and form
as we say the prayer of Jesus—
Our Father . . .

Bread and Cup
(Spoken and performed by a worship leader or leaders)

The bread we break
is our communion in the body of Christ.

The cup we share
is our communion in the blood of Christ.

Come to the light of the world,
the bread of life,
the fountain of living water.
All is ready. Come!

Communion

Prayer after Communion
(Spoken by a worship leader or in unison)

Living God, Holy One, Holy Three,
thank you for feeding us at this table.
As we go, keep us close to you,
trusting in your love,
and bearing the good news of Jesus Christ,
in whose name we pray.
Amen.

There Never Was a Time[2]

A Trinitarian Poem for Meditation and Reflection

(Spoken by one or more people. The refrain is printed in bold.)

There never was a time
when the Author had a thought
and then the Word was spoken
upon the Spirit's breath,
but endlessly from always
the Author freely speaks,
the Word is gladly spoken,
the Spirit freely moves:
You are the Three who are the One
who are the Three who are the One
forever.

There never was a time
when the Source began to rise
to send the Living Water
that tumbles from the Spring,
but endlessly from always
the Living Water shows
the beauty of the Wellspring,
the fullness of the Source:
You are the Three who are the One
who are the Three who are the One
forever.

Seeking, saving, sin forgiving,
reconciling and inspiring,
making, tending, recreating,
finding, freeing, and uniting:
You are the Three who are the One
who are the Three who are the One
forever.

Yet you created time
and the earth in starry space,
and journeyed with your people,

2. Brian Wren. Copyright © 2001 by Praise Partners Publishing (Brian Wren and Susan Heafield). For music, see Susan Heafield and Brian Wren, *Tell the Good News!—Worship Songs: Easter, Before and After,* distributed by Hope Publishing Company, Carol Stream, Illinois 60188, http://www.hopepublishing.com/. The refrain printed here is slightly altered from the original.

and opened Mary's womb;
and Jesus, filled with Spirit
to show the Source of love,
was crucified among us,
and raised, and so we know:
**You are the Three who are the One
who are the Three who are the One
forever.**

(Repeat ad lib.)

CHAPTER 10

Worship Elements for the
New Year and for Epiphany

New Year's Eve and Day
(Sunday or Not): Years A, B, and C

RCL READINGS: ECCLESIASTES 3:1–13; PSALM 8; REVELATION 21:1–6A; MATTHEW 25:31–46

Two Hymns by Brian Wren

Sing Praises Old and New [1]

POETIC METER: 6.7.6.7.6 6 6.7.

Sing praises old and new,
   past and present join in one.
Old covenants renew:
   new commitments have begun.
God's soaring purpose spans
   all ages, lives, and lands.
Christ's open, wounded hands
   past and present join in one.

Word, from the heart of God,
   costly, unexpected grace,
Love, making all things good,
   Light of all the human race,
hail, Wisdom deep and vast,
   shining in Israel's past,
raising the least and last:
   costly, unexpected grace!

Great Spirit, make us wise,
   doors of promise open wide.
When evil's deadly lies
   truth and goodness set aside,
faith never stands alone,
   hope rolls away the stone,
love makes your presence known.
   doors of promise open wide.

---

1. Brian Wren. Copyright © 1993 by Hope Publishing Company for the USA, Canada, Australia, and New Zealand, and by Stainer & Bell for all other territories. All rights reserved. Used by permission.

People of hope, be strong!
   Love is making all things new.
Lift our united song,
   show what faith can dream and do!
Come, Presence ever near,
   revive us, year by year,
sing through our joy and fear.
   Love is making all things new!

This Is a Day of New Beginnings[2]

POETIC METER: 9.8.9.8.

This is a day of new beginnings,
time to remember, and move on,
   time to believe what love is bringing,
   laying to rest the pain that's gone.

For by the life and death of Jesus,
love's mighty Spirit, now as then,
   can make for us a world of difference
   as faith and hope are born again.

Then let us, with the Spirit's daring,
step from the past, and leave behind
   our disappointment, guilt, and grieving,
   seeking new paths, and sure to find.

Christ is alive, and goes before us
to show and share what love can do.
   This is a day of new beginnings;
   our God is making all things new.

(*Alternative stanza 4, at communion*)

*In faith we'll gather round the table
to show and share what love can do.
This is a day of new beginnings;
our God is making all things new.*

(*Anyone who legally has this book may speak these poems aloud from it. To access the music and obtain permission to reproduce words or music, read the copyright information on p. ix.*)

2. Brian Wren. Copyright © 1983, 1987 by Hope Publishing Company for the USA, Australia, and New Zealand, and by Stainer and Bell for all other territories. All rights reserved. Used by permission.

Worship Elements for New Year's Eve and Day

Before We Speak

A Call to Worship

(Spoken by a worship leader or leaders, or by worship leader[s] and congregation. The responding or congregation voice is printed in bold.)

Before we speak, God is here,
within us and among us, knocking at our door.
Living God, open what is closed
that the Spirit may come in.
Open our hands, to give, and to greet.
Open our minds
to new truth and old wisdom.
Open our hearts to new hope and old assurance.
Open what is closed
that the Spirit may come in.

Before God

A Petition

(Spoken by a worship leader or leaders, or by worship leader[s] and congregation. The responding or congregation voice is printed in bold.)

Living God, Holy Trinity,
before whom the generations rise and pass away,
to whom all life is an open book,
you search us and know us,
yet never control us.
Your Spirit prays for us
with sighs too deep for words.
Thank you for the signs of your presence—
within or through others:
a nudge, a call, a vision,
encouragement, rebuke, and unexpected wisdom.
Show us how to live our lives before you,
in your presence, your absence,
and everything in between,
through Jesus Christ,
your ever-present Word.
Amen.

Hinge of History

A Litany of Praise for the New Year and Anytime

(Spoken by a worship leader or leaders, or by worship leader[s] and congregation. The responding or congregation voice is printed in bold. Use in whole or in part. Option: sing the "Hallelujah!" using a well-known "Hallelujah/Alleluia!" from a hymn or service music in your hymnal or worship book.)

Living Christ,
hinge of history,
center of hope,
human face of holiness,
executed by the powers of this world,
raised beyond mortality,
alive among us:
> with heart and mind and voice
> **we praise you!**
> **"Hallelujah!"**

Before all worlds,
before time and space exploded into being,
before there was a "before,"
you shine,
offspring of the Origin,
expression of eternity:
> with heart and mind and voice
> **we praise you!**
> **"Hallelujah!"**

Before we were born,
you grew inside your mother's womb,
were delivered, cradled, nursed,
experienced childhood and youth,
were baptized, filled with the Spirit,
and proclaimed the good news of God's new world:
> with heart and mind and voice
> **we praise you!**
> **"Hallelujah!"**

Before we were schooled in dominance and submission,
you washed your disciples' feet.
Before we absorbed the worship of force
and the praise of revenge,
you practiced forgiveness and peace.
Before we learned the ways of the world,
you walked in the light of new creation:

And so,
with heart and mind and voice
we praise you!
"Hallelujah!"

Before we knew your name,
your Spirit sighed through our longings,
moved us to seek you,
and guided our search:
with heart and mind and voice
we praise you!
"Hallelujah!"

Somewhere on our journey
you met us.
With a whisper or a shout
you call us.
You are our hope and our joy,
and nothing in death or life,
in the world as it is or the world as it shall be,
nothing in all creation
can separate us from your love.
And so,
with heart and mind and voice
we praise you!
"Hallelujah!"

But Faith in Christ Declares

A Scripture-Based Affirmation of Faith

(Spoken by a worship leader or leaders, or by worship leader[s] and congregation. The responding or congregation voice is printed in bold. Use whole or in part.)

The world says, "Evil has always existed, and only force can
overcome it,"
but faith in Christ declares,
In the beginning when God created the heavens and the
earth, . . .
God saw everything that God had made,
and indeed, it was very good.
[But] sin came into the world . . . and death came through
sin.

(Gen. 1:1, 31 and Rom. 5:12*)

The world says, "Let the righteous destroy the wicked,
that justice may be done,"
but faith in Christ declares,
  There is no one who is righteous, not even one. . . .
  All have sinned and fall short of the glory of God.
                                                    (*Rom. 3:10, 23*)

The world says, "Violence is golden
when it is used to put evil down,"
but faith in Christ declares,
  The Living God tests the righteous and the wicked,
    and . . . hates the lover of violence.
  The fruit of the righteous is a tree of life,
    but violence takes lives away.   (*Ps. 11:5 and Prov. 11:30*)

The world says, "Lock them up and throw away the key,"
but the risen Christ declares,
  Blessed are the merciful,
  for they will receive mercy.
  Beloved, never avenge yourselves, . . . for it is written,
  "Vengeance is mine, I will repay, says the Living God."
                                            (*Matt. 5:7 and Rom. 12:19*)

The world says, "We have to murder and kill and destroy
to preserve everything that's good,"
but faith in Christ declares,
  Love your enemies
  and pray for those who persecute you.
  Blessed are the peacemakers,
  for they will be called children of God.
                                              (*Matt. 5:44 and 5:9*)

Alpha and Omega

A Call to Worship or Affirmation of Faith Drawn from Revelation
21:1–6a

*(Spoken by a worship leader or leaders, or by worship leader[s] and congregation. The
responding or congregation voice is printed in bold.)*

As the earth orbits the sun,
year follows year,
and century follows century,
we meet to worship God:
**You are the Alpha and the Omega,
the beginning and the end.**

As life follows life,
civilizations rise and fall,
empires descend to dust,
and generations pass away,
You are the Alpha and the Omega,
the beginning and the end.

Here and now, we live in the light of your promise
to dwell with us as our God
and wipe every tear from our eyes:
You are the Alpha and the Omega,
the beginning and the end.

Here and now, we live in the light of your promise
that death will be no more;
and mourning and crying and pain will be no more,
for the first things have passed away.
You are the Alpha and the Omega,
the beginning and the end.
Amen.

Never a Time to Hate

A Collect Prompted by Ecclesiastes 3:1–13

(Spoken by a worship leader or leaders, or by worship leader[s] and congregation. The responding or congregation voice is printed in bold.)

Jesus, Word in flesh appearing,
in your life among us
there was a time to be born, and a time to die,
a time to laugh, and a time to weep,
a time to speak, and a time to be silent,
a time for peace, but never a time for war,
a time to heal, but never a time to kill,
a time to love, but never a time to hate.
Govern your church,
that day by day and year by year,
we may measure our life by your life
and follow your distinctive way
in your name. Amen.

Christ in Glory

A Collect Prompted by Matthew 25:31–46

(Spoken by a worship leader or in unison)

Christ in glory,
whose standard of judgment
is not correctness but compassion,
move us by your Spirit
that we may work together
to prevent hunger,
house the homeless,
care for people who are injured and ill,
visit prisoners,
and welcome strangers
in your name. Amen.

New Creation

A Collect Based on 2 Corinthians 5:16–20

(Spoken by a worship leader or in unison)

Christ our hope,
reconciling us to God,
and giving us the ministry of reconciliation,
walk with us through time,
that amid the orbits of our planet
we may know, believe, and rejoice
that in you we enter a new creation,
where everything old has passed away
and everything has become new,
by your Spirit and in your name. Amen.

Lifting the Name of Christ

A Charge to the Congregation

(Spoken by a worship leader or leaders, or by worship leader[s] and congregation. The responding or congregation voice is printed in bold.)

Alive in Christ, let us live in Christ,
and lift the name of Christ with love,
not as a sword
but as a cross.

Let us use the name of Christ with care,
not as a hammer for hammering
but as bread for sharing.
Let us speak the name of Christ with praise,
not as a battle cry
but as a love song.

Lawgiver, Word, and Breath

A Trinitarian Blessing

(Spoken by a worship leader or leaders, for any time of year or following the charge above)

May the Giver of Law
the Word of Grace,
and the Breath of Life, One God,
help us to love justice, trust love,
and live faithfully,
through Jesus Christ, our Teacher, Friend, and Savior.
Amen.

Epiphany: Years A, B, and C

RCL READINGS: ISAIAH 60:1–16; PSALM 72:1–7, 10–14; EPHESIANS 3:1–12 ; MATTHEW 2:1–12

Introduction

It is hard to privatize Epiphany. Isaiah hails the divine light that dispels darkness over nations and peoples and brings exiles home. The psalm praises One who legislates peace, social justice (righteousness), and deliverance from oppressive violence. Ephesians heralds a divine mystery now to be revealed to "rulers and authorities" whose heavenly location parallels events on earth. Matthew shows "wise" men naive enough to ask a despot for travel directions to his successor. As always, we see the light most clearly when we name and meet the darkness.

An Epiphany Hymn by Brian Wren

Anyone who legally has this book may speak this poem aloud from it. To access the music and obtain permission to *reproduce* words or music, follow the copyright information on p. ix.

Will You Come and See the Light?[3]

POETIC METER: 12.12.14.10.

Will you come and see the light from the stable door?
 · It is shining newly bright, though it shone before.
　It will be your guiding star; it will show you who you are.
Will you hide, or decide to meet the light?

Will you step into the light that can free the slave?
　It will stand for what is right. It will heal and save.
　By the pyramids of greed there's a longing to be freed.
Will you hide, or decide to meet the light?

Will you tell about the light in the prison cell?
　Though it's shackled out of sight, it is shining well.
　When the truth is cut and bruised, and the innocent abused,
will you hide, or decide to meet the light?

3. Brian Wren. Copyright © 1993 by Hope Publishing Company for the USA, Canada, Australia, and New Zealand, and by Stainer and Bell for all other territories. All rights reserved. Used by permission.

Will you join the hope, alight in a young girl's eyes,
   of the mighty put to flight by a baby's cries?
   When the lowest and the least are the foremost at the feast,
will you hide, or decide to meet the light?

Will you travel by the light of the babe newborn?
   In the candle lit at night, there's a gleam of dawn,
   and the darkness all about is too dim to put it out:
will you hide, or decide to meet the light?

Worship Elements for Epiphany

Through an Infant Child[4]

A Call to Worship Drawn from Isaiah 60, Psalm 72, and Matthew 2

(*Spoken by a worship leader or leaders*)

Let us worship God.
Darkness covers the earth,
and thick darkness, the peoples.
The poor cry out for bread,
and the weak suffer violence.
But God's light shines
through an infant child.
We have seen his star at its rising
and have come to pay him homage.
He is like showers that water the earth,
like rain that falls on the mown grass.
Thanks be to God!

Come and Meet a Mystery[5]

A Call to Worship Drawn from Ephesians 3

(*Spoken by a worship leader or leaders*)

Come and meet a mystery,
hidden from the dawn of time,
now revealed among us.
Come and hear good news:
Christ has boundless riches.

---

4. First published in the *Abingdon Worship Annual 2005: Contemporary and Traditional Resources for Worship Leaders*, ed. Mary J. Scifres and B. J. Beu (Nashville: Abingdon Press, 2005), Epiphany Sunday.
5. Ibid.

Everyone may share them.
Say to all the people,
to rulers and authorities:
No one is discarded.
Everyone is welcome. Alleluia!

The World's True Light

A Call to Worship

(Spoken by a worship leader or leaders)

"Christ is the world's true light,
its captain of salvation,
the daystar clear and bright,
desire of every nation."[6]

We assemble in the name of Christ our Savior,
head of the church,
foundation of salvation,
hinge of human hope,
who chooses to be centered
not in the circles of privilege and power
but at the margin,
with the downtrodden, the rejected, and the despised.

We shall tell the story of God's mighty work in Christ
and offer our worship and praise.
Let us worship God.

Like a Bright Star

A Call to Worship

(Spoken by a worship leader or leaders, or by worship leader[s] and congregation. The responding or congregation voice is printed in bold.)

We meet to worship God
and to remember, tell, and show God's love.
Like a bright star in the night sky,
the life of Christ lights up the whole world.
The star of hope shines on,
and no darkness will overcome it.

---

6. The quotation is from the first stanza of "Christ Is the World's True Light," by G. W. Briggs.

The light of Christ shows us
who we are and what we can be,
where we have been and where we should go.
Let us walk in the light and give thanks to God.

Shine upon Us

A Call to Worship and Short Prayer Drawn from Matthew 2

(Spoken by a worship leader or leaders, or by worship leader[s] and congregation. The responding or congregation voice is printed in bold.)

When a child is born, light shines.
When Jesus is born, hope dawns
and love arrives.

**Newborn Jesus, shine upon us.
From your cradle and your cross
give us love and life.**

When the Light of God Shines[8]

A Call to Worship from Isaiah 60

(Spoken by a worship leader or leaders, or by worship leader[s] and congregation. The responding or congregation voice is printed in bold.)

When the light of God shines,
we shall see it and be radiant.
Our hearts shall thrill and rejoice!
**Glorious God, shine in our hearts
and fill us with praise.**

Not from a Palace[9]

A Collect Drawn from Matthew 2

(Spoken by a worship leader or in unison)

Toddler Christ, whose light shines out
not from a palace
but from a village woman's lap,
shine on us today

---

8. First published in the Abingdon Worship Book (2003) and copyright © 2003 by Brian Wren.
9. Ibid.

through the youngest and the least,
that we may open our treasures
and give them precious gifts
in your name. Amen.

The Cradle of Your Vulnerability

A Prayer of Confession and Lament Drawn from Matthew 2 and
Psalm 72

(Spoken by a worship leader or in unison)

Holy God, we confess and lament
the violence of our world
and our fascinated bondage
to military might,
merciless justice,
self-righteous revenge,
and national pride.
Shine on us
from the cradle of your vulnerability
that forgiveness, mercy, and kindness
may glow and grow among us
through Jesus Christ. Amen.

Within a Span of Time

A Prayer of Thanksgiving

(Spoken by a worship leader—not suitable for unison speech)

Living God, you have created us to live within a span of time.
Each of our lives is a bright thread in the tapestry of life,
unfolding over centuries.
Because we live in time, we can learn from the past
and give to the future.
So we thank you for the light that shines from the past:
in the discoveries and achievements of countless people,
in heroic deeds and in unsung acts of love.
Most of all we thank you for making yourself known to us;
for taking the time
to reveal yourself to the world,
and for the long unfolding of your revelation.
Today we thank you above all
for the shining light of Jesus Christ.

You have always known that light,
but to us it burst into history
like a new star in the night sky.
So we celebrate the epiphany of your love
and pray that the light of Christ
may shine on us, every day. Amen.

Nothing Is Hidden

A Petition

(Spoken by a worship leader or leaders, or by worship leader[s] and congregation. The responding or congregation voice is printed in bold.)

Holy and Loving God,
when your light shines, nothing is hidden;
and when your light shines on us,
there is joy in seeing
and discomfort in being seen.
Help us, by your love,
to bear the light of your truth and your integrity,
your forgiveness and your faithfulness.
Bring us out of hiding,
that we may become children of light,
through Jesus Christ,
the Light of the World. Amen.

Prayers in Response to Matthew's Whole Story—Matthew 2

In Year A of the RCL the Gospel reading for the first Sunday after Christmas has Matthew's account of the *departure* of the wise men and Herod's massacre of the children (Matt. 2:13–23), probably because its commemoration traditionally falls on December 28. Two weeks later, at Epiphany, the wise men *arrive* with their gifts (Matt. 2:1–12)! Thus, followers of the Revised Common Lectionary never hear Matthew's complete narrative, which is significantly different from that of Luke, for example, in its emphasis on divine guidance through dreams and in its portrayal of the wise men as having taken two years to reach their destination (see Matt. 2:16), so that they kneel before a two-year-old toddler, not an infant's manger. Whatever we make of Matthew's account, it deserves to be heard as a whole, in the order its author narrates, either as one continuous reading or in two parts (vv. 1–12 and 13–23). Here are two prayers in response:

Source of All Wisdom

A Collect

(Spoken by a worship leader or in unison)

> Living loving God,
> Source of all Wisdom,
> thank you for the spiritual leaders of another faith
> whose belief in the influence of stars
> took them on a two-year journey
> to find the child Jesus
> and pay him homage;
> lead us on new journeys
> so that in faiths that are foreign to us
> we may seek your presence
> and be ready to share our treasures
> in your name. Amen.

Toddler Christ [10]

A Collect

(Spoken by a worship leader or in unison)

> Toddler Christ,
> before whom wise men knelt
> after they had foolishly aided a tyrant
> who wanted to destroy you:
> make us, in the face of dangerous power,
> as crafty as snakes
> and as harmless as doves,
> so that we know when to be silent,
> when and how to speak,
> and when to take another road,
> in your name. Amen.

---

10. Try using this collect and pairing Matthew's narrative with 1 Corinthians 1, especially vv. 18–25.

Go Out as One Body[11]

A Blessing

(Spoken by a worship leader or leaders)

Go out as one body,
Christ's body.
Love.
Forgive.
Show mercy.
Make peace.
And tell the good news
of Christ, the world's light. Amen.

People of God, Go Out[12]

A Blessing

(Spoken by a worship leader)

People of God, go out!
Cradle in your hearts
the great mystery
of reconciling love,
that it may take root and flourish,
within you, among you, and beyond you,
through Jesus Christ. Amen.

11. First published in the *Abingdon Worship Book* (2003) and copyright © 2003 by Brian Wren.
12. Ibid.

Appendix

It Came upon the Midnight Clear (original text)

-1-

It came upon the midnight clear,
   that glorious song of old,
from angels bending near the earth
   to touch their harps of gold;
"Peace on the earth, goodwill to men,
   From heaven's all-glorious King."
The world in solemn stillness lay
   to hear the angels sing.

-2-

Still through the cloven skies they come
   with peaceful wings unfurled,
and still their heavenly music floats
   o'er all the weary world;
above its sad and lowly plains
   they bend on hovering wing,
and ever o'er its Babel sounds
   the blessed angels sing.

-3-

But with the woes of sin and strife
   the world has suffered long;
beneath the angel-strain have rolled
   two thousand years of wrong;
and man, at war with man, hears not
   the love song which they bring:
O hush the noise, ye men of strife,
   and hear the angels sing!

-4-

And ye, beneath life's crushing load,
   whose forms are bending low,
who toil along the climbing way
   with painful steps and slow,
look now! For glad and golden hours
   come swiftly on the wing:

O rest beside the weary road
and hear the angels sing!

-5-
For lo! the days are hastening on
by prophet-bards foretold,
when with the ever-circling years
comes round the age of gold;
when peace shall over all the earth
its ancient splendors fling,
and the whole world give back the song
which now the angels sing.

A full discussion is in my book *Praying Twice: The Music and Words of Congregational Song* (Louisville, KY: Westminster John Knox Press, 2000), 341–45.

Index of Scripture Sources

Index of Topics and Themes